The Darwinian Genocide in Africa

The Darwinian Genocide in Africa

*Darwinian Influences in the Development of
Supremacist and Segregationist Policies in Africa*

JERRY BERGMAN

foreword by David V. Bassett

preface by Paul Gosselin

WIPF & STOCK · Eugene, Oregon

THE DARWINIAN GENOCIDE IN AFRICA
Darwinian Influences in the Development of Supremacist and Segregationist Policies in Africa

Wipf & Stock
An Imprint of Wipf and Stock Publishers
199 W. 8th Ave., Suite 3
Eugene, OR 97401

www.wipfandstock.com

PAPERBACK ISBN: 979-8-3852-6987-7
HARDCOVER ISBN: 979-8-3852-6988-4
EBOOK ISBN: 979-8-3852-6989-1

VERSION NUMBER 02/17/26

Contents

Foreword

AFRICA HAS HISTORICALLY BEEN described as "The Dark Continent" due to the limited knowledge of Europeans of its interior during their nineteenth and twentieth-century era of expansion and colonization of the second largest continent on Earth. Though this moniker was born out of European ignorance, it was European arrogance that made it so. It was the prideful, self-exaltation of European "elites" thinking of themselves as evolutionarily "superior" in comparison to Africa's indigenous people groups—thusly designated as "inferior," "primitive," "savages"—that excused, in their own minds, all manner of European atrocities and humanitarian crimes against native Africans. This seeming justification of mass genocides, in keeping with the "might makes right," "the end justifies the means," "survival of the fittest" application of godless evolutionism, is well-documented and captivatingly clarified by the expert analysis of prolific author Dr. Jerry Bergman.

Masquerading as European "enlightenment," the darkness of Darwinian dogma descended upon Africa as violent exploitation and savage subjugation decades before its satanic shadow returned to blacken Europe with the horrors of the Holocaust. Predating Hitler, Germany was responsible for the Herero and Namibian genocides of 1904–1907, as well as those later in Rwanda. The Belgians then took over terrorizing Rwanda after their King Leopold II victimized the African Congo from 1885–1909. Meanwhile, the British were wreaking havoc in Nigeria from the mid-nineteenth to the mid-twentieth centuries, the same time period that the French were causing chaos from West Africa all the way to Madagascar. Even South Africa was not immune from European tyranny during the last century.

Dr. Bergman spotlights each of these calamities attributed ultimately to the embracement and implementation of the evolutionary, death-driven ethics of Darwinian eugenics. But there is plenty of blame to share. Where was the Christian church—the true "light of the world"—during these past two centuries of "race hatred," when it was supposed to be standing up to and defeating "evil-ution"? It was apparently choosing to be impotent as it compromised with unscriptural beliefs and actions, thereby allowing the influx of Darwinian dogma to metastasize into the rampant genocides throughout Africa, just as it permitted the eugenic venom of the "Final Solution" to infiltrate Nazi Germany. Dr. Bergman pulls no punches in this powerful publication. The bottom line is history does indeed, unfortunately, repeat itself when God's truth is unheeded and biblical lessons go unlearned.

David V. Bassett, MS

Preface

AMONG MOST EDUCATED WESTERNERS, offering a serious critique of Darwin by major publishers is unusual. Yet some of the greatest social catastrophes in the West, such as the Nazi Holocaust or the massive genocides occurring under Communism (the Holdomor in Ukraine, the Soviet Gulag, and the Chinese Laogai), were due to Darwinian influence. Both ideological systems applied the Darwinian "survival of the fittest" concept to modern societies. In the case of Nazism, the "survival of the fittest" concept was applied via conflict between races, whereas among communists, it was applied to conflicts between social classes (capitalists versus proletariat). After World War II, evolutionist Sir Arthur Keith made a point regarding Nazism that was soon forgotten:

> The German Fuhrer, as I have consistently maintained, is an evolutionist; he has consciously sought to make the practice of Germany conform to the theory of evolution. . . . To see evolutionary measures and tribal morality being applied vigorously to the affairs of a great modern nation, we must turn again to Germany of 1942. We see Hitler devoutly convinced that evolution produces the only real basis for a national policy. . . . The means he adopted to secure the destiny of his race and people were organized slaughter, which has drenched Europe in blood. . . . Such conduct is highly immoral as measured by every scale of ethics, yet Germany justifies it; it is consonant with tribal or evolutionary morality. Germany has

reverted to the tribal past, and is demonstrating to the world, in their naked ferocity, the methods of evolution.[1]

Before World War II, the great majority of social scientists were promoters of scientific racism, and their works provided both inspiration and justification for the oppressive policies Bergman describes below. In my university days, a professor was introducing students to Claude Levis-Strauss's structural anthropology perspective and pointing out that this perspective contributed to push back against the racist idea that members of so-called "primitive societies" were incapable of rational thinking. Yet my professor never reflected on the reason why such racist ideas had become so embedded in the social sciences.

Few educated Westerners seriously reflect on the hard lessons of the twentieth century. In the following pages, Bergman forces the reader to look at the facts of Darwinism's impact in Africa during the colonial period as well as after World War II. Most Western intellectuals have left such *unpleasant* issues ignored, buried in colonial archives. Bergman doesn't let us get away with that.

While Darwin's works did contribute to racist views in the West, such views were already widespread before he wrote anything. This derives from the fact that the Enlightenment concept of "progress," when applied to nations or civilizations, inevitably leads to categorizing peoples according to their degree of "progress." This then leads to despising those with less technology or military power by those with more. It comes to no surprise, then, that the main contributor to South Africa's racist Apartheid regime was Cecil Rhodes, founder of the Oxford University Rhodes scholarship program. The openly racist subtitle to Darwin's most famous work, the *On the Origin of Species by Means of Natural Selection, or the Preservation of Favoured Races in the Struggle for Life* offers proof of how commonplace concepts such as *superior* and *inferior* races had already become before 1859. Yet, Darwin's writings amplified the dissemination of racist views and clothed

---

1. Keith, *Evolution and Ethics*, 27–28.

them in the prestige of *science*, largely, until recently, shielding them from critique.

One issue raised by Professor Bergman's chapter on the Rwandan genocide in the 1990s, exposing how Darwinian concepts poisoned relations between Hutus and Tutsis, is that such social violence is now becoming possible in the United States, as ideologies such as Critical Race Theory sow conflicts between different cultural groups (Blacks/Whites). Like nineteenth and twentieth century racist ideologies, woke racism sets up cultural groups as irreconcilable enemies. It seems naïve to think "It couldn't happen here."

In 2007, I taught at an Evangelical seminary in Brussels, Belgium. I was asked to do a weeklong seminar. That week, regular classes were suspended, and all students had to take the seminar associated with their program. In my case, I did one segment on the Origins debate and another on postmodernism. I had a very international group of students: one-third Europeans, one-third Asians, and one-third Africans.

European students had a very muted reaction to my critique of the theory of evolution in the Origins segment. On the other hand, African students had a *very* enthusiastic reaction to my critique of evolution. After reading Professor Bergman's book, I now realize that the African student's enthusiastic reaction to my critique of evolution was rooted in living memories of the brutal oppression by colonial officials, which was openly justified by Darwinian propaganda. For generations, Africans were condescendingly (and brutally) reminded of their "inferior" status. In contrast, the Bible's teaching rejects the concept of "race" and exposes the fact that we are all family. That said, the dark events of human history expose the grim fact that the fallen sons of Adam and the fallen daughters of Eve constitute a very dysfunctional family.

Paul Gosselin, MA
Social anthropologist, author, webmaster (samizdat.qc.ca)

Acknowledgments

THE NUMEROUS SCHOLARS THAT made this book possible include Mark Amber, whose paper on South Africa I had the privilege of extensively editing, providing much insight on the situation there.

I also must thank Paul Gosselin, MA; educator Steve Sobek, BS; Ted Siek, PhD; Douglas Sharp, BS; Kevin Wirth; Kirk Toth, MS; David Bassett, MS; Carl Baugh; Richard Geer; and my wife, Dianne Bergman, who was supportive of my four-years' work researching the material for this book.

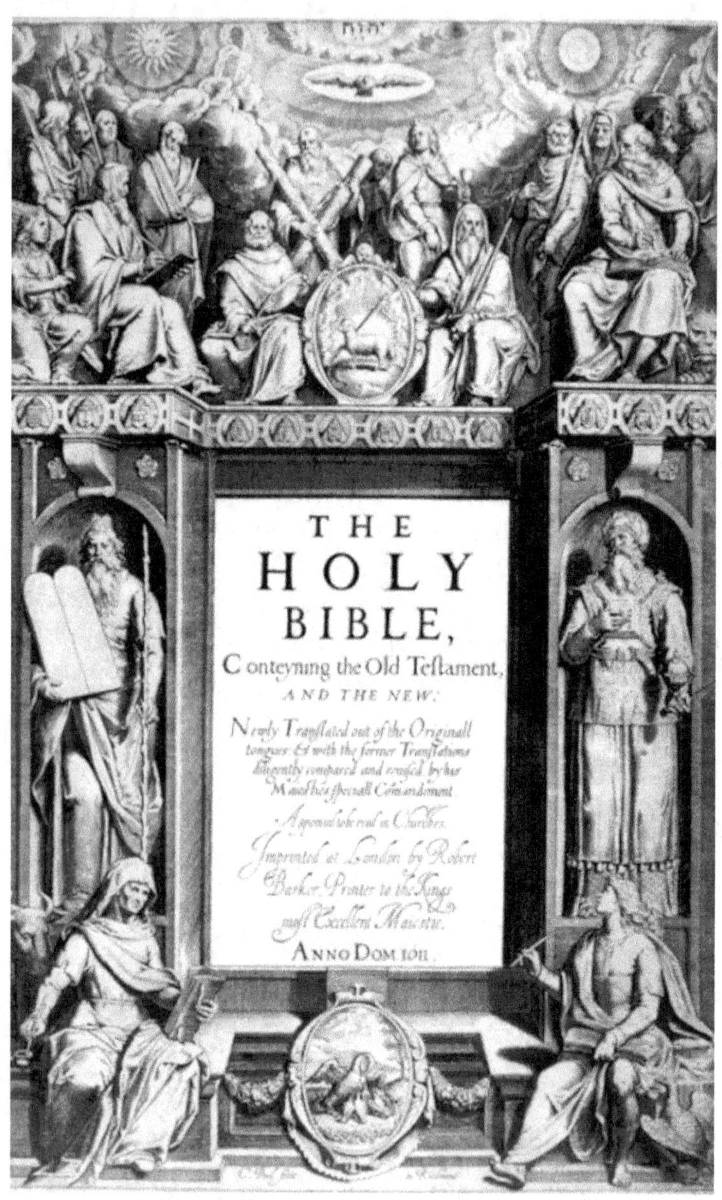

1611 English translation of the Christian Bible

1

The Bible on War and Peace

ONE EVENT THAT LED to the genocide in Africa was the widespread acceptance of the Darwinian worldview by the large Christian denominations. One example is that the Dutch Reformed churches were racially mixed for decades. This changed as evolution permeated society and, consequently, permeated the churches. The large churches were gradually divided into separate Black and White congregations. By 1921, Darwinian language and ideas began to be used in Dutch Reformed Church documents to justify racism. One example was, "'the laws of evolution and heredity' which ensured that Africans could not immediately 'attain to the moral stature of those who have generations of Christian forebears behind them.'"[1]

Eventually, biblical teaching on racial equality motivated many Christians to take a stand against the racism that dominated their society. Nonetheless, it had a profound influence on Africa.

Of note is that the online complete works of Darwin includes a content warning for readers that the material "on the Darwin Correspondence Project website may include content and language that is upsetting or offensive. . . . This can include language that is racist, sexist, . . . and otherwise discriminatory and unacceptable today."[2]

1. Dubow, *Scientific Racism*, 252.
2. Darwin Correspondence Project, "From William Henry Harvey."

Unfortunately, too few accepted the biblical view to play a major role in resisting social Darwinism that was then being pushed on many European nations. Albert Luthuli, the first Black African man to receive the Nobel Peace Prize, stated in his autobiography that Christianity belongs to every race and nation because

> the Christian faith sprang from Asia Minor, and to this day it speaks with a Semitic voice. Western civilization is only partly Western. It embraces the contribution of many lands and many races. It is the outcome of interaction, not of apartheid. It is an inheritance, something received to be handed on, not a white preserve. I claim with no hesitation that it belongs to Africa as much as to Europe or America or India. The white man brought it here, originally, but he brought a lot of other things too.[3]

The "other things" were largely the ideas that were infected with Darwinism that swept the Western world from the late nineteenth century onwards. The churches, many which accepted Darwinism, ignored the fact that *Darwin himself went through the transformation that Darwinism has wrought on millions of people.* When Darwin

> returned from five years at sea, Darwin still believed in a wonderous creation. It took him more than twenty years . . . to complete an outline of a theory that decisively shifted modern consciousness to the realities of a world in which divine intervention played no part. Life and death belonged to nature; the cause of life and death could be construed as rational, natural, and even moral within nature's harsh amoral laws.[4]

In his travels to South America, Darwin became aware of events involving Whites slaughtering the indigenous people, who were only attempting to defend their lands against expropriation. Darwin recognized that the Whites were, in his words, on a mission to exterminate the native people. One event Darwin discussed involved "112 women and children and men [who] were 'nearly all

3. Luthuli, *Let My People Go*, 47.
4. Moses and Stone, *Colonialism and Genocide*, 23.

taken or killed, very few escaped."[5] In the ensuing struggle with a native, a soldier stated, "I . . . struck him with my sabre to ground, then got off my horse & cut his throat." Darwin responded that to him [Darwin] this act appeared rather inhuman. The solder answered Darwin by asking him, "Why is it inhuman?" noting "what can be done, they breed so."[6] "Like wild animals however, they fight to the last instant."[7] All the women who appeared above twenty years old were massacred in cold blood.[8] Darwin added that for females below age twenty, "the children of the Indians are saved, to be sold or given away as a kind of slave, for as long a time as the owner can deceive them."[9]

Darwin noted the natives did not have a chance against the well-armed and well-trained British army. Darwin commented that only "one Christian was wounded" in the struggle with the indigenous natives.[10] Darwin's reaction was not horror about the natives that were ruthlessly slaughtered, as it would be to most Americans, but rather his concern was about the perpetrators of the slaughter.[11]

> The killing was reasonable and even moral in the larger scheme of things. Everyone here is fully convinced that this is the justest war, because it is against barbarians.[12]

Darwin recognized, as normal people do today, that a problem with this event is that these atrocities were committed in a civilized Christian country. He rationalized this obvious evil by stating,

> If this war is successful, that is if all the Indians are butchered, a grand extent of country will be available for

5. Keynes, *Charles Darwin's Beagle Diary*, 180.

6. Keynes, *Charles Darwin's Beagle Diary*, 180.

7. Keynes, *Charles Darwin's Beagle Diary*, 179.

8. Keynes, *Charles Darwin's Beagle Diary*, 180.

9. Keynes, *Charles Darwin's Beagle Diary*, 180.

10. Moses and Stone, *Colonialism and Genocide*, 24.

11. Keynes, *Charles Darwin's Beagle Diary*, 177, 179.

12. Keynes, *Charles Darwin's Beagle Diary*, 180.

the production of cattle, and the vallies . . . will be most productive of corn. The country will be in the hands of white Gaucho savages instead of copper-coloured Indians. The former being a little superior in civilization, as they are inferior in every moral virtue.[13]

Darwin added that "General Rosas's plan is to kill all stragglers & thus drive the rest to a common point.—In the summer, with the assistance of the Chilians, they are to be attacked in a body, and this operation is to be repeated for three successive years"[14] until the native Indians are all extinct. Darwin added, "Summer is chosen as the time for the main attack, because the plains are then without water, & the Indians can only travel in particular directions."[15] Those words were written in 1833 in Darwin's notebooks, and he summarized in his book published in 1845 what happened during the Indian conflict that he wrote about earlier:

> Not only have whole tribes been exterminated, but the remaining Indians have become more barbarous: instead of living in large villages, and being employed in the arts of fishing . . . they now wander about the open plains.[16]

The following chapters in the book you are now reading allow us to look back in history, in historian Arnold's words, at the "faults, excesses and atrocities [that were] committed in the name of racial Darwinism, eugenic imperialism, and fascism: [atrocities that now] have been admitted, [for which] forgiveness [has been] sought, and [for which] massive reparations [have been] paid" by the European countries and are still being paid.[17]

13. Keynes, *Charles Darwin's Beagle Diary*, 181.

14. Keynes, *Charles Darwin's Beagle Diary*, 180.

15. Keynes, *Charles Darwin's Beagle Diary*, 180.

16. Darwin, *Journal of Researches*, 104.

17. Arnold, *Imperial Atrocities*, 400.

AFRICA AS THE ORIGIN LOCATION OF HUMANS

Another reason for the genocide of Black Africans is that the majority of missing links connecting human evolution to our putative hominid ancestors were found in Africa, and it is implied that Black Africans were less evolved than Whites. As a result of subscribing to the now thoroughly discredited "recapitulation" theory of Ernst Haeckel, Professor Raymond Arthur Dart and University of Cape Town physical anthropologist Matthew Drennan all believed that modern-day Bushmen were "anatomical curiosities or living fossils" that "lie towards the simian end of the human scale. . . . The Bushman is undoubtedly a member of one of the lowest of the meaning races."[18] One conclusion of the intelligence testing was that the *adults* of "inferior" races were equal in intelligence to the children of "*superior*" races.

Darwin believed that the origin of humans was in Africa, supporting the idea that the native African people were less evolved than the White races. They concluded the Bushmen were "soon to be added to the many dead branches of already extinct forms."[19] This belief inspired many evolutionists to search for evidence of human evolution in Africa, "the cradle of mankind." Australian anatomist and anthropologist Raymond Arthur Dart (1893–1988), professor of anatomy at the University of Witwatersrand, claimed that his 1924 discovery of the Taung skull (*Australopithecus africanus*) was the most important fossil ever discovered."[20] Since then, hundreds of fossil fragments have been uncovered in Africa.

FAILURE TO APPLY CHRISTIANITY LEADS TO THE AFRICAN GENOCIDE

Most of the accounts recorded in this book involved people from European Christian nations committing brutal genocide against non-Christian native Africans. Both the Hebrew and Greek

18. Dubow, *Scientific Racism*, 49.

19. Dubow, *Scientific Racism*, 49.

20. Dubow, *Scientific Racism*, 44.

Scriptures condemn all war, including those that result in genocide, except defensive war. The horrible examples of man's inhumanity against man documented in this book by persons identifying as Christians result in the Christians-against-non-Christians scenario often used by atheists and persons opposed to Christianity to condemn Christianity. In fact, the problem is not Christianity but rather not conforming to or living according to clear Christian teaching.

The King James Version (KJV) uses the word "peace" 429 times, and the New International Version uses it only 230 times. Conversely, the word "love" is used in the KJV 310 times, and the New Living Translation uses it 801 times. The KJV uses the word "forgive" 95 times; the English Standard Version uses it 109 times. The words "Christian," "peace," "love," and "forgiveness" are synonymous, such as in the phrase "He is not behaving very Christian." Unfortunately, secularization of society has also occurred in the churches; thus, these central biblical themes need to be stressed even more today than in the past.

These ideals are clearly central biblical themes, regardless of which translation is used. Much has been written by leading historians and scholars about the Christian scriptural attitude toward war that documents the position outlined above.[21] A few of the many biblical examples of teaching against war and instead teaching the values of peace are listed below.

KEY SCRIPTURES ON WAR AND PEACE

Note, all Scriptures in this section are taken from the Christian Standard Bible.

> *Isaiah 2:4*: He will settle disputes among the nations
> and provide arbitration for many peoples.
> They will beat their swords into plows
> and their spears into pruning knives.
> Nation will not take up the sword against nation,
> and they will never again train for war.

21. Bainton, *Christian Attitudes*.

Isaiah 9:6: For a child will be born for us,
a son will be given to us,
and the government will be on his shoulders.
He will be named Wonderful Counselor, Mighty God,
Eternal Father, Prince of Peace.

Psalm 11:5: The Lord examines the righteous,
but he hates the wicked
and those who love violence.

Psalm 34:14: Turn away from evil and do what is good;
seek peace and pursue it.

Proverbs 15:1: A gentle answer turns away anger,
but a harsh word stirs up wrath.

Deuteronomy 32:35: Vengeance and retribution belong to me.
In time their foot will slip,
for their day of disaster is near,
and their doom is coming quickly.

Micah 4:3: He will settle disputes among many peoples
and provide arbitration for strong nations
that are far away.
They will beat their swords into plows
and their spears into pruning knives.
Nation will not take up the sword against nation,
and they will never again train for war.

Matthew 5:9: Blessed are the peacemakers,
for they will be called sons of God.

Matthew 5:21–24: You have heard that it was said to our ancestors, Do not murder, and whoever murders will be subject to judgment. But I tell you, everyone who is angry with his brother or sister will be subject to judgment. Whoever insults his brother or sister will be subject to the court. Whoever says, "You fool!" will be subject to hellfire. So, if you are offering your gift on the altar, and there you remember that your brother or sister has something against you, leave your gift there in front of the altar. First go and be reconciled with your brother or sister, and then come and offer your gift.

Matthew 5:43–44, 47–48: You have heard that it was said, Love your neighbor and hate your enemy. But I tell you, love your enemies and pray for those who persecute you. And if you greet only your brothers and sisters, what are you doing out of the ordinary? Don't even the Gentiles do the same? Be perfect, therefore, as your heavenly Father is perfect.

Matthew 6:14: For if you forgive others their offenses, your heavenly Father will forgive you as well.

Matthew 18:21–22: Then Peter approached him and asked, "Lord, how many times must I forgive my brother or sister who sins against me? As many as seven times?" "I tell you, not as many as seven," Jesus replied, "but seventy times seven."

Mark 11:25: And whenever you stand praying, if you have anything against anyone, forgive him, so that your Father in heaven will also forgive you your wrongdoing.

Romans 12:17–21: Do not repay anyone evil for evil. Give careful thought to do what is honorable in everyone's eyes. If possible, as far as it depends on you, live at peace with everyone. Friends, do not avenge yourselves; instead, leave room for God's wrath, because it is written, "Vengeance belongs to me; I will repay," says the Lord.
"But If your enemy is hungry, feed him.
If he is thirsty, give him something to drink.
For in so doing you will be heaping fiery coals on his head."
Do not be conquered by evil, but conquer evil with good.

1 Peter 4:8: Above all, maintain constant love for one another, since love covers a multitude of sins.

The best example is in the Ten Commandments, the one that says "Thou shalt not kill," which is the central goal of war. Wars are won by killing as many of the enemy as possible and destroying their property until they sue for peace. Only then does the killing and destroying end.

A Note on the Commandment

Many Bible-believing Christians do not believe the commandment "thou shalt not kill" applies to killing someone who has unrighteously taken the life of another person. The Bible is clear that the state is to apply capital punishment for such cases (Gen 9:5–60; Exod 21:12–14). In addition, perhaps a similar argument can be made for the case of a defensive war or for the killing of someone who is about to murder someone else.

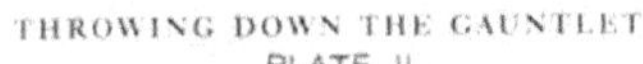

An example illustrating the anti-Black racism in book illustrations.

The first illustration (Plate II) contrasts the white man and the obviously inferior African negro and shows the similarity of the Black African and other apes. The second illustration (Plate III) of the skeletons was to better illustrate the ape traits of the Black Africans by showing the skeletons of each of the figures. Notice in the second illustration the Black African looks very apelike.[22]

Nineteenth-century engraving of Black African slaves being transported across the Sahara Desert to North Africa.[23]

22. From Hawkins, *Comparative Anatomy*.

23. From Wikimedia Commons: https://commons.wikimedia.org/wiki/File:Arabslavers.jpg.

2

The Problem of Darwinism

Genocide in Africa

IN THE 1800S AND early 1900s, tens of thousands of Europeans journeyed to Africa to steal African wealth and, under the penalty of death, force the native people to become the slaves of their conquerors. When some of the African people resisted, the Europeans retaliated with a level of brutality previously unknown in Europe or Africa. The Africans' hand-held weapons were futile against the Europeans' powerful guns and cannons, which they used to produce a ruthless slaughter never before seen by the African people. The result was close to a million indigenous inhabitants murdered, and millions more were maimed, blinded, or had their hands and feet severed. The Europeans stole land and wealth from them because they thought that the native people were less than human or, at the least, were a primitive, backward people lacking civilized culture.

The focus of this book is that, besides greed, the main justification for the African genocide was the social Darwinian belief that the Africans were biologically and culturally inferior to the Europeans. If a Frenchman were to decide that he wanted the material wealth of a German, and he traveled to Germany to take what he wanted, both French and German societies would condemn him and take steps not only to stop him but also to punish him. This is because the offender and the offended are both White Europeans.[1] The same behavior, however, was often considered acceptable when White Europeans came to Africa and began stealing, looting, and abusing the native people, most of whom were Black or dark brown. At the very least, the White Europeans often got away with their crimes because Black Africans were widely considered by White Europeans to be an inferior race and culture.

In Europe, land is owned by someone or, if not, it belongs to the state. African land, they assumed, was not owned by anyone but, in short, was there for the taking. However, in fact, the native people actually did, by tradition, recognize land ownership.

Acceptance of the Genesis teaching that Adam and Eve were the parents of all people living today, White and Black, negates the belief that Blacks are less-evolved than Whites, which was the main excuse for Europeans to plunder the lands and people of Africa. The problem was that the teaching of Genesis was often ignored by the plunderers. In contrast, the Christian missionaries who accepted Genesis along with the biblical teaching about loving your neighbor opposed the brutality and, eventually, after much struggle, forced it to end.[2] One result has been the conversion of over half of Africa to Christianity. Indigenous religions are now practiced by very few people, although most northern Africans are Muslim.[3]

1. *The Chicago Manual of Style*, which *The Darwinian Genocide in Africa* generally follows, has changed its recommendation since 2020 regarding the use of lower case "white" and "black" when these terms refer to racial or ethnic identities. *Chicago* now recommends capitalization of "White" and "Black" in light of recent and ongoing events and the evidence of a real shift in usage across many sources. However, these terms do not designate races. Only a single race exists: the human race.

2. Mathews, *Book of Missionary Heroes*; Oluniyi, *Darwin Comes to Africa*.

3. Johnson and Crossing, "Religions by Continent."

THE DARWINIAN BASIS FOR BELIEF
IN INFERIOR RACES

Darwin first addressed in detail the topic of human evolution and race in his 1871 book *The Descent of Man*, conclusively documenting Darwin's brutal racism and his belief in White supremacy. In the *Descent* book, Darwin applied his theories of natural selection to humans. He describes Australians, Africans, Mongolians, Indians, South Americans, Polynesians, and even Eskimos as inferior races of "savages." Actually, he considered every non-European, non-White population to be inferior savages.

Darwin constantly elevated White Europeans in every way as better than "savages." He explained that the "highest races and the lowest savages" differ in "moral disposition . . . and in intellect."[4] He used the word "savage" or "savages" a whopping 116 times in his 1871 book. The belief that White people are more intelligent, more moral, and more evolved persists throughout the rest of his book. Darwin further described what he meant by savages, describing them as having "low morality," "insufficient powers of reasoning," "confinement of sympathy to the same tribe," and "weak power of self-command."[5] Darwin linked his belief in White supremacy with his theory of natural selection, by which he justified violent imperialism to abuse savages. Quoting Darwin, "From the remotest times successful tribes have supplanted other tribes. . . . At the present day, civilized nations are everywhere supplanting barbarous nations."[6]

Darwin's specific claims about the major deficits in the intellectual capacities of "savages" are alarming. He begins with the animals: "No one supposes that one of the lower animals reflects whence he comes or whither he goes,—what is death or what is life."[7] He then extended these conclusions to humans, stating, "How little can the hard-worked wife of a degraded Australian

4. Darwin, *Descent of Man*, 35.
5. Darwin, *Descent of Man*, 97.
6. Darwin, *Descent of Man*, 160.
7. Darwin, *Descent of Man*, 62.

savage, who uses hardly any abstract words and cannot count above four, exert her self-consciousness, or reflect on the nature of her own existence?"[8] His perspective on non-European races is not only incredibly prejudiced but, at times, absurd. Darwin claims that Australians and other savages are incapable of complex thought and insinuates that they are in many ways very much like the lower animals.

Darwin's theory applies the "survival of the fittest" philosophy to human races. He wrote that the extermination of non-White races is a natural consequence of the superior and more successful race of White Europeans. Furthermore, Darwin justified violently overtaking other cultures as expected, even normal, because it has happened regularly throughout natural history. He seemingly had no problem with continuing the vicious behavior of past generations. At least, he never condemned this behavior.

Not only did Darwin believe in White supremacy, but he offered a biological proof for it, namely that White people are more evolved than non-Whites. He writes that the "western nations of Europe, . . . now so immeasurably surpass their former savage progenitors and stand at the summit of civilization."[9] As White Europeans "exterminate and replace" the world's "savage races," just as great apes go extinct, Darwin writes, "At some future period, not very distant . . . the civilized races of man will almost certainly exterminate and replace throughout the world the savage races."[10]

The gap between civilized man and his closest evolutionary ancestor, the apes, Darwin taught, will widen as a result. The gap will eventually be between civilized man "and some ape as low as a baboon, instead of as at present between the negro or Australian and the gorilla."[11] Darwin believed that Africans and Australians were more closely related to the apes than to Europeans. In Darwin's

8. Darwin, *Descent of Man*, 62.
9. Darwin, *Descent of Man*, 178.
10. Darwin, *Descent of Man*, 201.
11. Darwin, *Descent of Man*, 201.

theory, modern humans are largely restricted to White Europeans, and all other races are viewed as somewhat subhuman.[12]

Many Darwin scholars and teachers venerate Charles Darwin and ignore this central component of his theory. Nevertheless, there are exceptions, such as Professor Rutledge Dennis, who examined Darwin's role in perpetuating scientific racism in *The Journal of Negro Education*.[13] He documented that the dark side of Darwin detailed above calls into question his prized intellect and legacy, observing that racism and discriminatory behavior follow directly from his theories.[14] Specifically, Dennis summarized Darwin's conclusions that "talent and virtue were features to be identified solely with Europeans."[15] White supremacy is clearly embedded in the heart of *The Descent of Man*, in spite of Darwin's alleged brilliance and the assumed validity of the rest of his theory.

FAILED ATTEMPTS TO NEGATE THE RACIST PART OF DARWIN'S THEORY

The enormous level of veneration for Darwin demands a response to his racist teachings, which were used to justify the century-long genocide that occurred in Africa. In spite of the fact that *The Descent of Man* clearly contains a racist and White supremacist ideology, Adrian Desmond and James Moore unsuccessfully argue against the idea that the core of Darwin's theory is racist. They even claim that Darwin studied evolution only to bolster the abolitionist cause: "Darwin's starting point was the abolitionist belief in blood kinship, a 'common descent.'"[16]

In response to the claims of Darwin's critics, Desmond and Moore opine that "the real problem is that no one understands Darwin's core project. . . . No one has appreciated the source of that

---

12. JBHE Foundation, "Blacks Less Likely," 39–40.

13. Dennis, "Social Darwinism," 243–52.

14. Anderson, "Dark Side of Darwinism."

15. Dennis, "Social Darwinism," 243.

16. Desmond and Moore, *Darwin's Sacred Cause*, xvii.

moral fire that fueled his strange, out-of-character obsession with human origins."[17] How can Desmond and Moore claim to know Darwin's mind? They reached their conclusions after an exhaustive search through "a wealth of unpublished family letters and a massive amount of manuscript material."[18]

Using these sources, Desmond and Moore attempted to make a case against the idea that Darwin was a racist, citing evidence such as the diary that Darwin kept during his *Beagle* voyage. In this diary, Darwin writes about slavery: "It makes one's blood boil, yet heart tremble, to think that we Englishmen and our American descendants, with their boastful cry of liberty, have been and are so guilty."[19] Darwin often wrote thoughts that didn't align with the ideas in *The Descent of Man*. The fact is, Darwin openly taught that the more successful races dominate the less evolved races was the law of nature. He speaks comfortably of White Europeans exterminating other races. He never once expressed outrage at the killing, based on race, that he discussed in graphic detail. And Desmond and Moore themselves admit, "Perpetrators of the worst atrocities have seen themselves as 'favored races' surviving Darwin's bloody 'struggle.'"[20]

Another argument made in favor of Darwin blames the time period in which he wrote, not Darwin. The *Journal of Blacks in Higher Education* states that "Darwin, like [Abraham] Lincoln, believed in white supremacy, but he was far more enlightened and sympathetic to blacks than most white men of his time."[21] The question of whether Darwin himself was a racist is separate from the question of whether his theory was racist. The text of *The Descent of Man* is undeniably racist, and most readers only engage with the text, not with what he wrote in his diary, whether his family supported abolition, or how much he interacted with African Americans. These details add to the understanding of the

17. Desmond and Moore, *Darwin's Sacred Cause*, xix.

18. Desmond and Moore, *Darwin's Sacred Cause*, xix–xx.

19. Desmond and Moore, *Darwin's Sacred Cause*, 183.

20. Desmond and Moore, *Darwin's Sacred Cause*, xix.

21. JBHE Foundation, "Blacks Less Likely," 39–40.

man, but *The Descent of Man* exists separate from its author and the context of its writing.

The Descent of Man was written long ago, and Charles Darwin is long dead. Darwin, and the context in which he wrote his theory are history, but the text lives on and will continue to exist as an independent entity. When determining if Darwin's theories contain racial ideology, the text cannot be softened or explained away with outside information, as Darwin apologists attempt to do. Our contemporary reverence for Darwin's gentlemanly qualities and his claimed scientific brilliance is an illusion that shatters on a closer look at his publications, especially, but not only, his *Descent of Man* volume.

ENTER EUGENICS

Charles Darwin's cousin Francis Galton carefully read the major books his cousin wrote and realized that we can use evolution to cause further evolution of humans. He coined the word "eugenics" in 1883, meaning "good genes" to improve humans. Darwin's son, Sir George Darwin, was a leader of the eugenics movement. He visited South Africa to support the South African eugenics movement.[22]

The goal of eugenics was to reduce in society unwanted or harmful traits that were believed to be hereditary. This goal was achieved by restricting the breeding of "undesirables" and promoting the breeding of "desirables." It was applied in Africa by condemning, or even outlawing, miscegenation of the White Europeans and the Black Africans. Besides condemning interracial marriage, both forced abortion and forced sterilization were employed to achieve eugenics' practice of culling the gene pool of undesirables, which reached its highest level in the Nazi death camps.[23]

22. Beinart and Dubow, *Scientific Imagination in South Africa*, 161.
23. Zubrin, *Merchants of Despair*.

MIXED-RACE MARRIAGES CONDEMNED

Many African countries under colonial rule attempted to prohibit, by law, or at least strongly condemn, interracial marriages between Black Africans and White settlers. For example, after World War I, mounting anxiety existed in African White circles

> over the possible threat to white racial purity through mixed-race reproduction called "miscegenation." Sarah Gertrude Millin's novels about mixed race marriage, such as *Dark Water* (1921) and *God's Stepchildren* (1924), illustrate this preoccupation with inter-racial sexual liaisons and the emergence of what eugenists claimed produced a degenerate "half-caste" progeny.[24]

It was widely believed that the offspring of what social Darwinists judged as a superior race and an inferior race would result in the gradual degeneration of the superior White race. Social Darwinists predicted intermarriage with the inferior race would "bring down" the quality of the superior race.

In 1927, the Immorality Act was passed by the South African parliament, outlawing sexual relationships across the color line to prevent miscegenation. Similarly, in September of 1935, the Law for the Protection of German Blood and German Honor was passed by Germany's parliament (the Reichstag) forbidding Aryans from having sexual relations with Jews.[25]

University of Witwatersrand Professor Harold B. Fantham supported banning interracial marriages and all sexual contact between Blacks and Whites to prevent the birth of offspring of mixed races. He also argued that the mentally unfit should be sterilized for the same reason. One "solution" practiced in Nazi Germany was to murder over ten million people. These policies were a necessary part of a campaign for what Professor Fantham termed a "eugenic conscience" in South Africa.[26] He also became very active in establishing numerous committees on genetics and eugenics in

24. Rich, "Race, Science, and the Legitimization" 676.
25. Dubow, *Scientific Racism*, 133.
26. Rich, "Race, Science, and the Legitimization," 675.

the *South African Association for the Advancement of Science* for the same reason.

This issue was not unique to Africa. In the United States, from the late seventeenth century onwards, many states and territories prohibited interracial marriage, often under the term "miscegenation." Also, often prohibited were interracial sexual relations.

These laws were rooted in racist and eugenic beliefs about racial purity and the supposed inferiority of certain, less evolved racial groups, mostly Blacks. These laws were not symbolic but were often actively enforced. Individuals who violated them were guilty of a felony and faced imprisonment, fines, or other penalties. In some states, ministers were by law prohibited from officiating interracial marriages.

It was only in 1967 when the Supreme Court, in a unanimous decision in *Loving vs. Virginia*, declared them unconstitutional. Consequently, interracial marriages were legal nationwide, and all laws against miscegenation were null and void. The Loving case involved Richard and Mildred Loving, a marriage between a biracial Native American Black woman and a White man.[27]

INTERRACIAL MARRIAGE IS BENEFICIAL

The claim that a claimed inferior race would "bring down" the quality of the superior race is not supported by science. In fact, interracial marriage tends to do the exact opposite. Even the appearance of the mixed-race marriage's offspring is often considered more attractive than the offspring of a non-mixed-race marriage.[28]

Computer research into the area of what traits makes an attractive female face combined several hundred faces, and the product was considered the most attractive.[29] Thus, deviations from average were less attractive. Researchers have repeatedly found that a composite of two different races, producing an average of

27. *Loving v. Virginia*, 388 US 1 (1967).
28. Latson, "Biracial Advantage"; Banks, "Mixed-Race Children and Families."
29. Little et al., "Facial Attractiveness."

the two faces, is consistently rated as more attractive than the individual faces used to create them. This finding has led to the conclusion that averageness is a key factor in attractiveness.[30]

Interracial marriage disproves the Darwinist and eugenic racial conclusions concerning humans. Race is a social construct, an idea based mostly on visual clues. The Scriptures are very clear. All humans are decedents of Adam and Eve; thus, there are no races, and all humans are the same race—the human race.[31]

MEDICAL REASONS SUPPORTING INTERRACIAL MARRIAGES

The clearest example of the advantages of interracial marriage is that many diseases are caused by two damaged recessive genes. If only one is damaged (i.e., mutated), the person is normal. Sickle-cell anemia is the best-known example. If the damaged gene from the mother and the same damaged gene from the father are inherited by their child, the disease results. This particular damaged gene is almost exclusively in the Black population. But in a child who is the offspring of an interracial couple, the sickle-cell disease is almost unknown. Among the one hundred thousand Americans with sickle-cell anemia, it's the most common life-shortening genetic disease in the United States. People who only inherit one mutated gene (hemoglobin S) from one parent are said to have the sickle-cell trait. They often have no, or minor, symptoms.[32]

Cystic fibrosis (CF) is the most common autosomal recessive disease found in the White population, specifically in Caucasians of Northern European descent. It affects about one in 2,500 to 3,000 Caucasians. CF is an autosomal recessive condition caused by mutations in the cystic fibrosis transmembrane conductance regulator protein, which functions as a chloride channel in epithelial cells. This protein is crucial for maintaining the balance of salt

30. Little et al., "Facial Attractiveness."

31. Yudell, *Race Unmasked*, 1.

32. Wonkam, "Perspectives in Genomics."

and water in the body, particularly in the lungs and other organs. Because this disease is very rare in the Black population, it is almost unknown in interracial marriages.[33]

AMERICAN BLACKS RECOGNIZE
THE HARM OF EVOLUTION

In a study reported in *The Journal of Blacks in Higher Education* (JBHE) that compared the acceptance of evolution by Whites in contrast to Blacks, concluded that

> American blacks are among the groups most likely to accept the biblical account of human origins. The strong religious beliefs of most African Americans appear to explain this. Undoubtedly, too, the rejection of Darwin by many black people is due to the racist elements present in much contemporary writings that use Darwin to support a thesis that blacks lack intelligence and imagination of whites.[34]

The JBHE report quotes public opinion researcher George Bishop, who published that "the vast majority of Americans of all races believe . . . *that God created man pretty much in his present form within the last 10,000 years.*"[35]

The JBHE report added that, historically, for various reasons some people

> call on the spirit of Charles Darwin to defend their beliefs in the genetic inferiority of black people. This group . . . have never surrendered the Victorian view that blacks are a step closer to the apes than are members of the Caucasian race. In 1881 E. A. Freeman, a professor of modern history at Oxford University, declared "America would be grand if only every Irishman would kill a Negro. Niggers resemble big monkeys dressed up for game, half-men and still more half-women, hideous

33. Gilbert et al., "Ethnic Intermarriage and Its Consequences."

34. JBHE Foundation, "Blacks Less Likely," 39.

35. Bishop, "Religious Worldview," emphasis added.

apes whom Darwin clearly has left unfinished" [meaning they have not evolved as far upward as whites].[36]

The JBHE report also stated that "Charles Darwin did indeed believe in the inferiority of the black race, . . . but unlike many of his scientific colleagues of his time, Darwin did not believe that blacks evolved separately from whites."[37] Darwin's position was that "all races of man were descended from the same primitive stock, . . . [and] over the ages the different races of man acquired different physical and mental capabilities."[38]

In other words, Whites evolved to a much higher level than Blacks, thus Blacks were less evolved and, as a result, "there will always continue to be a lot of bad biological science to sustain racial bigotry in the United States."[39] This view was the main excuse for Europeans to plunder the lands and people of Africa.

Acceptance of the Genesis teaching that Adam and Eve were the parents of all people living today, White and Black, negates the concept that Blacks are less evolved than Whites. Once God as creator is rejected, the next step is an attempt to answer the origin of the universe and everything in it, questions that have stymied the greatest minds in science. The answer, after decades of study, is the belief accepted by the majority of scientists today: evolution and the big bang.

36. JBHE Foundation, "Blacks Less Likely," 40.
37. JBHE Foundation, "Blacks Less Likely," 40.
38. JBHE Foundation, "Blacks Less Likely," 40.
39. JBHE Foundation, "Blacks Less Likely," 40.

Two men hold the severed hands of their countrymen who were murdered in 1904 by rubber sentries. The men on the side are missionaries who documented the atrocities in Congo during the colonial era in an effort to stop the genocide.[40]

40. Schomburg Center for Research in Black Culture, Jean Blackwell Hutson Research and Reference Division. "Natives of the Nsongo District (Abir Concession)." New York Public Library Digital Collections. https://digitalcollections.nypl.org/items/e19d09d0-c6bf-012f-feb3-58d385a7bc34.

3

The Darwinian Belgian Congo Holocaust

THE PUBLICATION OF CHARLES Darwin's *On the Origin of Species* (subtitled *Or the Preservation of Favoured Races in the Struggle for Life*) in 1859 had a devastating effect on society. The most well-documented example is Nazi Germany, but many other examples exist. Both Nazi Germany and the Congo Holocaust had their source in the writings of Charles Darwin and his colleagues:

> Hitler may have lost his mind, but all his ideas in *Mein Kampf* are based upon the leading philosophical and scientific knowledge of his day and before. The lineage from Malthus, Spencer, Darwin, and the Eugenics movement through Ernst Haeckel, Darwin's German popularizer and promoter of the myth of racial superiority is clear. A professor of Biology at Jena University, Haeckel's books sold in the millions. . . . Hitler certainly did assign different values to people's lives, exactly adopting Darwin's notion of "sub-humans" as he formulated his genocidal plans.[1]

As this chapter will document, Darwin also greatly influenced the White Europeans' perception of native Africans. In his chapter

1. Egan, "Hitler and the Social Construction," paras. 2–3.

titled "Darwinism and Racism," history professor William Cohen observed that the "introduction of Darwinist thought reinforced the doctrine of racial inequality," which dominated the white colonizers of Africa.[2] Furthermore, the convinced Darwinists "professed to base their beliefs in the doctrine of racial inequality on a reading of the English scientist."[3] Ms. Royer, the woman who translated Darwin's *On the Origin of Species* into French in 1862, was convinced that Darwin "proved the falseness of the doctrine of racial equality."[4] Darwin also influenced the Europeans' perception of the natives of Belgian Congo, a colony in Central Africa ruled by Belgium from 1908 to 1960, and before that by their king, Leopold II.[5] Only in 1960 did the colony gain independence, becoming Zaire and later the Democratic Republic of the Congo.

HISTORY OF THE HOLOCAUST

In the 1880s, the European powers were busy carving up Africa into colonies that they could control. Belgium's King Leopold II managed to seize for himself the vast and largely unexplored territory surrounding the Congo River. The 1884–1885 Berlin Conference awarded Leopold an almost one million-square-mile area of Congo in 1885.[6] He was the absolute ruler of this area from 1885 to 1908. Using Belgian state funding, he plundered the ivory, rubber, and mineral wealth from his personal African fiefdom.[7] Income from the plunder rose ten-fold from one hundred fifty thousand to eighteen million francs from 1890 to 1898.[8] In the end, King Leopold II's rule was a story of unmitigated evil.[9]

2. Cohen, *French Encounter with Africans*, 248.

3. Cohen, *French Encounter with Africans*, 248.

4. Cohen, *French Encounter with Africans*, 248.

5. Anstey, *King Leopold's Legacy*.

6. Hochschild, *King Leopold's Ghost*, 1.

7. Hochschild, *King Leopold's Ghost*, 3.

8. Dworkin, *Congo Love Song*, 9.

9. Ascherson, *King Incorporated*.

Under Leopold's rule, the Congolese people routinely had their hands and even feet cut off for failure to meet rubber collection quotas imposed on them by Leopold. To enforce his brutal rule, Leopold increased Belgium's military presence in Congo from 1,487 troops in 1889 to 19,028 in 1898.[10] Even after Leopold's rule, in Africa, "safety conditions in the mines were abysmal: in the copper mines and smelters of Katunga, five thousand workers died between 1911 and 1918."[11] Native women were held for ransom and the populations of entire towns were massacred. In the end, as many as ten million Africans perished from murder, disease, industrial accidents, famine, overwork, and starvation, making it one of the worst killing grounds of modern times. The exact number is unknown because the death toll "was incidental. Few officials kept statistics about something they considered so negligible as African lives."[12]

THE CENTRAL INFLUENCE OF SOCIAL DARWIN IN LEOPOLD'S RULE

Although little has been written in English about Leopold's philosophical ideas, he was unequivocally a product of his Darwinian age and was overtly supported by some outright Darwinists.[13] He was clearly a racist, a world view that dominated his behavior against the African Blacks.[14] The politics in this era was increasingly framed in the language of scientific racism. The racist policies of Darwinian race science could be more fully implemented in the colonies that were isolated from the Western public eye. In contrast, in Europe, with its Christianized culture, the application of racists ideas was more subtle and covert. Nevertheless, much

10. Dworkin, *Congo Love Song*, 9.

11. Hochschild, *King Leopold's Ghost*, 279.

12. Hochschild, *King Leopold's Ghost*, 225–26.

13. Dworkin, *Congo Love Song*, 9.

14. Anstey, *King Leopold's Legacy*.

of the war against the native Congo population was framed, and justified, in terms of race. As Whitaker R. Birt concluded,

> Colonization was simply the by-product of the entrenched European racism, and . . . it is used today to justify the actions of not only Belgium in the Congo, but European nations throughout Africa on the basis of a theory of cultural Darwinism premised upon the idea of "might makes right" and the "ends justify the means."[15]

Some colonists, as in the Congo, even employed a "scorched earth" survival-of-the-fittest strategy by burning farms and putting their wives and children into what amounted to concentration camps, where thousands died from disease and malnutrition.[16]

A major reason for the genocide in the Congo was that Leopold regarded Blacks as a less-evolved, savage race, clearly inferior to the Whites, that Darwin wrote would eventually become extinct. In fact,

> to Europeans, Africans were inferior beings: lazy, uncivilized, little better than animals. In fact, the most common way they were put to work was like animals, beasts of burden. In any system of terror, the functionaries must first of all see the victims as less than human, and Victorians' ideas about race provided such a foundation.[17]

For example, Leopold believed that "there is no question of granting the slightest political power to negroes. That would be absurd. The white men, heads of the nations, retain all the power."[18] The attitude of many of those who had the political power was "they shoot . . . negroes as if they were monkeys."[19] For punishment, "Whites were not put in irons, of course; only blacks [were]."[20] To save money, and not waste bullets, the Belgian military required

---

15. Nzongola-Ntalaja, *Congo from Leopold to Kabila*, 28.

16. Birt, *Congo*.

17. Scholz, *Phenomenon of Torture*, 102.

18. Hochschild, *King Leopold's Ghost*, 67.

19. Hochschild, *King Leopold's Ghost*, 51.

20. Hochschild, *King Leopold's Ghost*, 68.

one severed hand from each native for each bullet expended. Those who lost their hands for this reason included not only dead natives but also some who were still alive.[21]

Few textbooks today, for good reasons, openly teach racism, but it was very commonly taught in the past. Efforts to deal with Leopold's past include removing statues that honour Leopold because, "when it comes to ruthless colonialism and racism, few historical figures are more notorious than Leopold II."[22]

The first major scientist to openly teach racism was Charles Darwin. His racist worldview is even in the title of his most famous book, *On the Origin of Species by Means of Natural Selection, or the Preservation of Favoured Races in the Struggle for Life*. In Darwin's 1871 book, *The Descent of Man*, chapter 7 is titled "On the Races of Man" and contains forty pages that cover in detail his racist conclusions about humans.

Darwin concluded from his interactions with the Tierra del Fuego natives that it was hard to believe "how wide was the difference between savage and civilized man."[23] Darwin believed that the gap was

> greater than between a wild and domesticated animal. . . . Viewing such men, one can hardly make oneself believe they are fellow-creatures, and inhabitants of the same world. . . . At night, five or six human beings, naked and scarcely protected from the wind and rain of this tempestuous climate, sleep on the wet ground coiled up like animals.[24]

Darwin also wrote, in 1893, that in the future, "an endless number of the lower races will have been eliminated by the higher civilized races throughout the world."[25]

In South Africa, obscuring the role of Darwinian racism allowed intellectuals to cling to their evolutionary origins theory

21. Dworkin, *Congo Love Song*, 9.

22. Associated Press, "Belgium's Colonial-Era King."

23. Darwin, *Charles Darwin*, 238.

24. Darwin, *Charles Darwin*, 238.

25. Darwin, *Charles Darwin*, 69.

without the mark of racism. Modern "liberals" often choose to ignore the important role of science in the racist movements of Africa. The fact is, in South Africa at least, "mainstream biological scientific racism coincided with social imperialism and racial segregationist movements."[26]

Humans that Darwin concluded were clearly "inferior" to White Europeans included not only "Negroes" and Hottentots but also native New Zealanders and Australians. The "superior" races included the Europeans and those superior individuals that evolved by natural selection "from barbarians."[27] Darwin added that he believed the Hottentots were evolutionarily even lower than the "Negro," and "if it could be proved that the Hottentot had descended from the Negro, I think he would be classed under the Negro group, however much he might differ in color and other important characters from Negroes."[28]

DARWIN INFLUENCED TEXTBOOK WRITERS

The racism inspired by Charles Darwin, one of the most esteemed scientists that ever lived, greatly influenced science textbook writers. An example from geography is Adolph von Steinwehr's 1870 textbook titled *Primary Geography*. He wrote in lesson 12, titled "The Races of Men,"

> There are five races: . . . the white and the black, the red, the yellow, and the brown races. The white or Caucasian race is superior to all, and exceeds any other race. . . . The greater proportion of the civilized people live in Europe and America, and belong to the white race. They know more than other nations. This is the reason why they are more powerful, and live more comfortably.[29]

26. Rich, "Race, Science, and the Legitimization," 674–75.

27. Darwin, *Descent of Man*, 404.

28. Darwin, *On the Origin of Species*, 424.

29. Steinwehr and Brinton, *Primary Geography*, 16–19.

The author then concludes this section by discussing what he calls "the Savage, or uncivilized people" of Africa.[30]

Another leading geography textbook, *Eclectic Physical Geography* by Professor Russell Hinman, states,

> The mental development of . . . the woolly-haired and brown skin type . . . as a whole is lower than that of the other [racial] types. . . . All races of this type are native in the southern hemisphere, which is thus characterized in its human, as well as in its animal inhabitants, by a relatively low state of development. . . . [The] mental development [of the] straight-haired type of mankind . . . is higher as a rule than in the woolly-haired type.[31]

The last example cited here is from the textbook *Essentials of Geography: First Book* by Professors Albert Perry Brigham and Charles T. McFarlane.[32] The authors opine about Blacks that "most of the African natives are still savages and ignorant in spite of efforts made to educate them."[33]

The common belief in the inferiority of African "Negroes" compared to American "Negroes" was stated by Dr. Benjamin Hays:

> The superiority of the American negro to his African brother, who is a savage and cannibal [is because] at the dawn of history he [the African negro] was fully developed, and during the past three thousand years he has not made one step of progress. . . . He has shown no power to advance.[34]

Dr. Hays added that "history is one continuous record of the struggle between races.[35] . . . If the negro were in a position to make a contest for supremacy . . . the tragedy enacted with the

---

30. Steinwehr and Brinton, *Primary Geography*, 19.

31. Hinman, *Eclectic Physical Geography*, 359–61.

32. Brigham and McFarlane, *Essentials of Geography*.

33. Brigham and McFarlane, *Essentials of Geography*, 240.

34. Hays, "Natural Selection," 8.

35. Hays, "Natural Selection," 7.

Indian would be repeated."[36] The reason for the difference between the Whites and Blacks is evolution, namely, the struggle for existence as detailed by Charles Darwin.

EXTINCTION OF THE BLACK RACE

In his book *Exterminate all the Brutes*—brutes referring to Black Africans—Sven Lindqvist wrote, quoting Darwin, that the "improved and modified descendants of a species will generally cause the extinction of the parent-species."[37] In 1859, in a letter to Darwin's collaborator, Charles Lyell, Darwin gave an example of what he meant by these words, writing about "the less intelligent races being exterminated."

Lindqvist then elaborated, writing, "In the *Descent of Man* (1871), Darwin made public his conviction: 'Today between the primates and civilized man are intermediate forms such as gorillas and savages, but both of these intermediate forms are dying out.'"[38] He then quotes Darwin, who said, "At some future period, not very distant as measured by centuries, the civilized races of man will almost certainly exterminate, and replace throughout the world the savage races."[39] Lindqvist then documents that Darwin's writings had an enormous influence throughout the world, specifically in Africa, the home of the so-called "savage races."[40]

These claims today appear both unfounded and ignorant, as well as racist, yet they were widely believed in Darwin's day and help explain why so many well-educated persons became active in the Ku Klux Klan and other organizations that opposed basic civil rights for all Americans. Darwinian racist ideas were supported by most academics throughout the world prior to the late 1940s. For example, biological race theories continued to be promoted

36. Hays, "Natural Selection," 12.

37. Lindqvist, *Exterminate All the Brutes*, 106.

38. Lindqvist, *Exterminate All the Brutes*, 107.

39. Lindqvist, *Exterminate All the Brutes*, 107. Quoting Darwin, *Descent of Man*, 201.

40. Lindqvist, *Exterminate All the Brutes*, 106.

by some Afrikaans' academics, such as Professor P. J. Coertze, even after Leopold II's rule was overthrown.[41] Though less well documented, similar atrocities occurred in other rubber-growing countries in Africa under other colonial powers.[42]

THE END OF LEOPOLD'S REIGN OF TERROR

The Belgian Congo atrocity occurred in a colony of one of the first major industrial countries that had the means of spreading information about the genocide occurring there. The telegraph and cameras were especially effective in revealing the horrors occurring there to the rest of the world. Photographs of the atrocities showing native "workers" who had lost their hands or had been tortured were also very important in bringing this horrible treatment of the Congo natives to the world's attention.[43] The result was that the world, especially the clergy, responded aggressively to end the Congo holocaust.

Mark Twain published a politically satirical pamphlet in 1905 harshly condemning Leopold II's rule over the Congo Free State, which was especially effective.[44] Those who fought Leopold's exploitation of Africans also included a brave handful of missionaries, travelers, and young idealists who went to Africa for work or adventure, and unexpectedly found themselves witnessing a holocaust. Edmund Morel was a young British shipping agent who led an international crusade against Leopold. Two courageous Black Americans, George Washington Williams and William Sheppard, risked their lives to bring evidence of the Congo atrocities to the outside world. A young Congo River steamboat officer named Joseph Conrad was another example. Even the Archbishop

41. Dubow, *Scientific Racism*, 103.

42. Hochschild, *King Leopold's Ghost*, 280.

43. Morel, *King Leopold's Rule in Africa*.

44. Twain, *King Leopold's Soliloquy*. The monograph was also published in French, German, and Italian.

of Canterbury was active in condemning the treatment of Black Africans in the Congo.[45]

LEOPOLD AND HIS SUPPORTERS
FIGHT THE TRUTH

As opposition to his brutal rule in the Congo began to be publicized in the United States, University of Chicago anthropologist Frederick Starr, who was an ardent believer in the inferiority of "primitive" peoples, received one of Leopold's innumerable medals and a full-year, all-expenses-paid tour of the Congo. In return, he produced a series of fifteen enthusiastic articles in the *Chicago Daily Tribune* under the heading, "Truth About the Congo Free State,"[46] in which he functioned as an astute propagandist in favor of Leopold's nefarious activities.

Leopold's motives and genocidal activities eventually were exposed to the public. Leopold's reign of terror ended in 1908 when it became a colony, namely, the Belgian Congo. King Leopold died the next year. Unfortunately, neither the change in the name of the Congo nor the king's death ended the ongoing exploitation of the natives.[47] Only as opposition grew did it eventually end.

Science has now vindicated the teaching of the Bible and has rejected the racist teaching of evolutionism. The clear teaching of Genesis is that all mankind living today descended from Adam, thus no races exist because there is only one race, the human race.

45. Sindani, *Gestrandet im "Paradies,"* 79.

46. Hochschild, *King Leopold's Ghost*, 244.

47. Dworkin, *Congo Love Song*, 9.

"5,000 people seeking refuge in this house of God [Ntarama church] were killed by grenade, machete, rifle and burning alive."[48]

48. By Scott Chacon, Aug. 4, 2006, from Wikimedia Commons: https://commons.wikimedia.org/wiki/File:Ntrama_Church_Altar.jpg

4

The Rwandan Genocide

Inspired by Darwinism

INTRODUCTION

THE APRIL–JULY 1994 RWANDAN genocide illustrates how a single group of people living next door to each other, speaking one language and sharing the same culture, even intermarrying, can be artificially divided into two "races." The artificial division was done by colonial rulers infused with Darwinism. The "race" judged "superior" was the Tutsi race, and that judged "inferior" was the Hutu race. In the end, one of the worst genocides of the last century took the lives of close to one million Rwandans, mostly Tutsi murdered by Hutu using machetes, clubs, and small arms.[1]

The mass slaughter was openly committed by the civilian population, not the government or the military, as is true of most genocides. Furthermore, the international community stood by while a "million defenseless victims died," even though numerous "warnings of impending genocide were transmitted" to the people.[2] To end the genocide, well-armed foreign forces were flown

1. Jones, *Genocide*, 232.
2. Jones, *Genocide*, 232–33.

in, but only to help the Whites, not the Blacks.[3] The Tutsi "begged the foreign troops for protection," but they ignored their cries and left the country, allowing the genocide to continue unabated. Thousands of "Tutsi were massacred within hours of the foreign forces' departure."[4] Troops were sent in only after the genocide.

This is one more example of the harm that results from rejecting the biblical teaching that all humans are descendants of Adam and Eve and replacing this belief with Darwinism and the "more-evolved" and "less-evolved" belief structure of evolutionism. The fact is "creationism would only be challenged in the second half of the nineteenth century after the publication of Darwin's *On the Origin of the Species*."[5] In the century since Darwin, racial war has led to the murder of an estimated *one billion* innocent people.[6]

THE HUTU AND TUTSI

The two largest ethnic groups in Rwanda are the Hutu and Tutsi. The Hutu make up 85 percent of the population, and the Tutsi a mere 14 percent. Most of the remaining 1 percent of the population are Twa (a.k.a. Batwa, the pigmy hunters). Rwanda, a stunningly beautiful country, is located in the eastern part of central Africa. Rwanda is about the size of Maryland, as is Burundi, while the total combined population, as of 2025, for both Rwanda and Burundi is close to twenty-nine million, making Rwanda and Burundi the most densely populated nations in Africa.

Rwanda was first colonized by Germany in 1894. The German administration was infused with Darwinism, which it used to divide the people into two main racial groups. Germany became one of the first nations to be converted to Darwinism and soon spread this "survival of the fittest" worldview to their colonies. As early as 1871, Professor William Preyer wrote to Darwin explaining that

3. Jones, *Genocide*, 233.

4. Jones, *Genocide*, 233.

5. André, "Phrenology and the Rwandan Genocide," 278.

6. Panné et al, *Black Book of Communism*; Wikipedia, "List of Wars by Death Toll."

there is no University in Germany where your theory is so openly confessed and publicly taught by so many professors. Häckel, Gegenbaur, Dohrn, Strasburger, W. Müller, myself: we are true Darwinians, in our lectures and writings.[7]

From academia, Darwinism rapidly spread throughout Germany and then to its African colonies. The first colonizers

brought with them their obsession with the classification of human kind according to their race and origin. This Western Pseudo-Science was influenced by the work of Charles Darwin and his theory of evolution. Western settlers [from Europe] saw themselves as culturally superior to the savages they had discovered and were eager to document these three new found races [the Hutu, the Tutsi, and the Twa].[8]

After 1918, when the Germans lost World War I, they were forced to give up all of their colonies. As a result, the Belgians took over Rwanda. They used not only Darwinism but other factors, even the long-debunked phrenology belief, to infuse racial ideas into Rwanda, which eventually lead to the Rwandan genocide.[9] Although this review focuses on the importance of Darwinism, as is common in genocidal killings, several factors were involved.

The division, which resulted from the artificial racialization of Hutu and Tutsi in both Rwanda and Burundi, was a legacy of colonization that produced one of the most violent and bloody events anywhere in the modern world. It was only under colonial rule "that the people of Rwanda have classified themselves upon such rigid racial lines. . . . The West has played a leading role in contributing to the prevalence of racism in Rwanda in the last century."[10] Colonial rule converted minor tribal differences into distinct racial categories.[11] Before this racialization, the vari-

7. Darwin Correspondence Project, "From William Preyer."

8. Millar, "Racism in Rwanda," 1.

9. André, "Phrenology and the Rwandan Genocide."

10. Millar, "Racism in Rwanda," 1.

11. Hinton, *Why Did They Kill?*, 2, 5, 22, 23–24, 26, 29, 178, 212, 282, 283, 285.

ous tribal groups largely lived in harmony with each other. They shared the same Bantu language, lived side by side without any "Hutuland" or "Tutsiland," and even often intermarried.[12]

Professor Prunier detailed how the German and Belgian intellectuals created the myth of White racial superiority based on Darwinism. In doing so, they did not realize that this new social structure would ultimately lead to enormous bloodshed. When the White colonizers were in Rwanda, the Tutsis, as the "superior race," had ultimate control over what the Belgians saw as their civilizing mission. The social structure put into place in Rwanda cannot be understood outside the context of Western values. As powerful as the Tutsi were, or thought they were, after independence, the Tutsi remained at the top of the hierarchy supported by the West.[13]

In support of this conclusion, some leaders accepted the questionable belief that the Tutsi had migrated south from the horn of Africa. As "foreigners," they "were somehow a 'superior race.'" The result was that the Rwandans were fundamentally unequal: "Some people were born to rule and to exploit, while others were born to obey and serve."[14] As Melvern has documented, the idea that the Hutu and Tutsi were distinct races "originated with the English ... [after] 1859, the year that Darwin published *On the Origin of Species*."[15]

HISTORY OF THE RACIALIZATION

In Rwanda, the Hutu and the Tutsi were originally social constructs that largely reflected class and community position. The wealthier individuals who owned more cattle were called Tutsi, while those living in subservient positions, or of poorer economic status, were defined as Hutu. Minor genetic differences were due to the fact that the Tutsi arrived in this region of Africa later than the Hutu. Nonetheless, in precolonial society, the Hutu and Tutsi terms were

---

12. Prunier, *Rwanda Crisis*, 5.

13. Prunier, *Rwanda Crisis*.

14. Melvern, *People Betrayed*, 11–12.

15. Melvern, *People Betrayed*, 11–12.

fluid, and depending on the person's lot in life, one could gain or lose either status.

When the Belgian authorities arrived, however, these positions calcified and the complicated nuances of the earlier era were ignored, allowing the pseudoscientific notions of race to take a firm hold on the Rwandan people. The Belgians instituted a permanent, *de jure* (by right), bifurcation of the groups as racial divisions.

The fact that "it is frequently difficult to distinguish between Hutu and Tutsi" required exaggeration of features and looking beyond actual physical differences.[16] The question asked after the genocide was, "How could it [the genocide] happen that people, who had shared the history of the same state, and who could be distinguished neither by culture nor language, could behave in such a way?"[17] British philosopher Lord Bertrand Russell (1872–1970) observed that racism created by the colonists in Africa "was the most horrible and systematic extermination of a 'people' [along with] . . . the Nazi's extermination of the Jews."[18] The

> most infamous instance of the lethal process of manufacturing difference occurred in Nazi Germany. Drawing on everything from archaeological evidence to theories of race, the Nazis divided the population into a hierarchy of biosocial types with the Aryan race at the peak. Jews, in contrast, were placed at the bottom of the hierarchy and viewed as a dangerous source of contamination.[19]

Likewise, the same lethal process of manufacturing races between people groups occurred in Rwanda. In the early decades of Belgian rule, because the Europeans favored the Tutsi, most educational opportunities, administrative positions, and economic benefits went to them. This guaranteed resentment on the part of the Hutu.[20]

16. Hinton, *Why Did They Kill?*, 212.
17. Hinton, *Why Did They Kill?*, 212.
18. Melvern, *People Betrayed*, 21.
19. Hinton, *Why Did They Kill?*, 212.
20. Jean, "Rwandan Genocide."

OTHER IMPORTANT STEPS LEADING TO THE GENOCIDE

The Belgian colonizers viewed the Hutu as ignorant, vile, slaves by nature, and lacking in ambition. Hutu features were considered ugly and indicative of the inferior, less-evolved Negro. A 1925 colonial report describes the Hutu "race" as "generally short and thick-set with a big head, a jovial expression, a wide nose, and enormous lips."[21] The Hutu were further described as "extroverts who like to laugh and lead a simple life,"[22] just like the apes they resemble. The Twa race were labeled as being the most primitive of the three racial groups. They were described as "small, chunky, muscular, and very hairy; particularly on the chest. With a monkey-like flat face and a huge nose, he is quite similar to the apes whom he chases in the forest."[23]

In contrast to the "intrinsically inferior" Hutu and Twa, the Tutsi received much praise from their Belgian colonizers. During this period of social Darwinism, Belgian colonizers judged the Tutsi as the most-evolved ethnic group in appearance and intelligence as well as more closely related to the Europeans than the Hutu. For this reason, they were regarded as superior to the Hutu. In fact, the

> Europeans were quite smitten with the Tutsi, whom they saw as too fine to be "negroes." Since they were [believed to be] not only physically different from the Hutu but also socially superior, the racially-obsessed, nineteenth-century Europeans started building a variety of hazardous hypotheses on their "possible," "probable," or, as they soon became, "indubitable origins."[24]

The colonial minister in Rwanda was quoted in 1925 as saying that the Tutsi, also called the Batutsi, were of good racial stock that had none of the undesirable traits

21. Wamwere, *Negative Ethnicity*, 57.

22. Wamwere, *Negative Ethnicity*, 57.

23. Prunier, *Rwanda Crisis*, 6.

24. Prunier, *Rwanda Crisis*, 6–7.

of the Negro, apart from his color. He is very tall, 1.8 m at least, [even] . . . 1.9 m or more. He is very thin, a characteristic which tends to be even more noticeable as he gets older. His features are very fine: highbrow, thin nose and fine lips framing beautiful shining teeth. Batutsi women are usually lighter skinned than their husbands, very slender and pretty in their youth, although they tend to thicken with age. . . . Gifted with . . . intelligence, the Tutsi displays a refinement of feelings which is rare among primitive people. He is a natural born leader, capable of extreme self-control and calculated goodwill.[25]

In short, the Belgians believed that Tutsi were "superior" to the Hutu primarily because they judged them to look more like the Belgians. Largely on this basis, the Tutsi were chosen by the Belgians to rule over the Hutu.[26]

In 1933, the racialization of Rwanda took one very important step in leading to the genocide: namely, the formal establishment of three races from what was formerly one people group. The Belgian administration organized a census that utilized the Belgian bureaucrats' terms to classify the entire population either as Hutu, Tutsi, or Twa. Every Rwandan was classified by such traits as height, nose length, and even eye shape. This is an example of the "almost obsessive preoccupation with 'race' in the late nineteenth-century anthropological thinking, [and] this peculiarity soon led to much theorizing . . . and at times plain fantasizing."[27]

The major problem, by far, with the Belgian bureaucrats' classification, as was also true in Nazi Germany, was that for

many Rwandans, it was not possible to determine ethnicity on the basis of physical appearance. Rwandans in the South were generally of mixed origin and most Rwandans of mixed origin were classified as Hutu. Yet many people looked typically Tutsi—tall and thin. In the north, mixed marriages were rare. Some people were given a

---

25. Belgium Ministère des affaires africaines, *Rapport sur de l'administration belge*, 34. Quoted in Twagilimana, *Debris of Ham*, 34.

26. Sinema, *Who Must Die*, 55.

27. Prunier, *Rwanda Crisis*, 5.

Tutsi card because they had more money or possessed the required number of cows.[28]

THE MASSACRE BEGINS

In spite of this problem, when the slaughter began, "Belgium portrayed the violence as a problem of race between the Hutu and the Tutsi."[29] From April to July 1994, the Hutu massacred over eight hundred thousand Tutsi and their Hutu sympathizers. After reviewing all of the common explanations for the genocide, including economic, political, and social, Prunier concluded that *a major factor* was the Darwinian worldview, due to the Belgian control of Rwanda, which divided the native people into groups based on their perception of race. The Belgian race distinctions, which were emphasized by the Belgians for decades, became firmly ingrained in the Hutu belief system. These beliefs later morphed into jealousy toward the Tutsi, which was then transformed into the rage of 1994. Although other factors were involved in the genocide, this review focuses on the major importance of Darwinian teaching that the Belgian government had implanted into the population. For example, the Hutu elite used the idea that another Tutsi invasion of their country might occur as a proactive justification for ethnic cleansing. The ethnic mythology made genocide a fathomable solution. The history of the conflict that caused what amounted to a civil war is, for very good reasons, often compared to the Nazi Holocaust.[30]

28. Melvern, *People Betrayed*, 14.

29. Melvern, *People Betrayed*, 17.

30. Hinton, *Why Did They Kill?*

A chart prepared to identify the Hutu from the Tutsi, which reflects the stereotype created by the Westerners. This chart reminds one of the stereotypes used by the Nazis to demean Jews during WWII.[31]

Just as the Nazis spoke of Jews as vermin living in alien bodies, eternal blood-suckers, parasites, and a plague that threatened to destroy the German state, so also the Hutu spoke of the Tutsi in similar terms.[32] Thus, reducing them to subhumans, calling them cockroaches and snakes, made their elimination appear to be critical for Hutu survival:[33]

> In Kangura, issue 40, the editorial title said it all: "A cockroach cannot bring forth a butterfly." The editorial argued that the Tutsi, like a cockroach, use the cover of darkness to infiltrate; "the Tutsi camouflages himself to

31. André, "Phrenology and the Rwandan Genocide," 280. Use is granted for the image if attribution is provided.

32. Hinton, *Why Did They Kill?*, 285

33. Hinton, *Why Did They Kill?*, 285.

commit crimes." This was not just one member of the group. All Tutsi men, women and children were no longer citizens of a nation but cockroaches. In the same way, all Tutsis were gradually associated with being spies of the Rwanda Patriotic Front (RPF)—Inyenzi—qualifying as enemies to be killed. . . . The killing of more than one million people was . . . carefully planned and executed. The dehumanization was an essential part of it.[34]

Although the Rwandan people did not have a specific term for race, when asked to explain the differences between Hutu and Tutsi, most commonly, the "respondents cited a physical characteristic such as height or skin color," the same criteria used to define race in the West.[35]

Professor Uzonna Anele claims that the influence of France was also critical in producing the genocide:

> One of the worst genocides in world history, claiming 800,000 lives of ethnic Tutsis in Rwanda, rests on the shoulders of France. Historians, human rights organizations, and other observers have reported that the French supplied arms to the Hutus after the "turquoise operation" [a French-led military operation] launched on June 23, 1994. French journalist Patrick-Exupery, claims that his country had launched this operation to reinforce the armament of Hutu groups.[36]

He claims part of the problem was that France did not create a secure zone to prevent the slaughter as they had promised. Furthermore, the fact that the

> observation mission in Rwanda by the *International Federation for Human Rights*, Jean Carbonare, denounced French colonial intervention in Africa, sounded the alarm. In particular, he warned about the "organized policy" of "ethnic extermination and human crimes" in which France was involved through military and

34. Ndahiro, "Dehumanization," paras. 6–7, 26.

35. Straus, *Order of Genocide*, 129–30.

36. Anele, "These African Countries," paras. 24–25.

financial support to the Rwandan government at that time.[37]

These accusations were denied by Former Minister for Europe and Foreign Affairs of France Hubert Vedrine, who felt that the main problem was that France failed to stop the spiral of civil war occurring between 1990 and 1994 in Rwanda.[38]

THE "CHRISTIAN" RACE THEORY

Many people in Rwanda, despite it being considered a Christian nation, rejected several of the core teachings of Christianity, including the teaching that all humans are one race, all descendants of the first couple, Adam and Eve. An early influential European, the English explorer and officer in the British Indian army, John Hanning Speke (1827–1864), even propounded the Hamitic hypothesis in 1863, in which he proposed that the lighter-skinned Tutsi ethnic group were descendants of the biblical figure Ham.[39] This was because they supposedly had more Hamitic features than the Bantu Hutu, over whom they ruled.

Speke postulated the idea that the Tutsi were a "conquering superior race." Speke derived his racist views from a faulty biblical interpretation of the Gen 9 story of Noah and his son Ham. Ham saw his father drunk and, as a result, God cursed him. Consequently, the claim is that Ham and his progeny, the Hamites, were cursed with dark skin.[40] Noah's other two sons' progeny, however, the theory teaches, were to father the Aryan and Semitic races. Unfortunately, some Christians also accepted this now thoroughly disproved Hamitic race theory and ignored the clear biblical teaching on race.[41]

37. Anele, "These African Countries," para. 26.
38. Anele, "These African Countries."
39. Maitland, *Speke.*
40. Sinema, *Who Must Die,* 55–56.
41. Burrell, "Slavery, the Hebrew Bible," 742.

SUMMARY

The "Belgians created a race distinction between two peoples where none had previously existed. Speke's race theory in action later led to a manufactured race struggle."[42] The end result of replacing the biblical teaching of race with the Darwinian view was a genocide that cost over one million lives. How two races were created from one people group that shared the same culture, language, and often intermarried is a lesson on how an idea can become a divisive legality, at least in the minds of the population. Nonetheless, the existing culture had set the stage for the racist division that resulted in the Rwandan genocide:

> European rule did not invent the terms *Hutu* and *Tutsi*, but the colonial intervention changed what the categories meant and how they mattered. . . . In the Rwandan Tutsi, the European explorers and missionaries believed that they had found a "superior" "race" of "natural-born" rulers. Europeans wrote that the Tutsi had . . . come to dominate the lowlier Hutu, which the Europeans considered an inferior "race" of Bantu "negroids." . . . This conception of Rwandan society reflected the anthropological ideas of the day, in particular the so-called "Hamitic hypothesis," which saw civilization in Africa as the product of "Caucasoid" (white-like) Hamitic peoples.[43]

In the end, false claims of racial differences were some of the most important factors in the Rwandan genocide. This is illustrated by the fact that the required "Rwandan national identity cards listed whether each cardholder was a Hutu, Tutsi, or Twa," solidifying a racial identity in the minds of each card carrier, most of whom were adults.[44] Also critical was that the contrived "idea that the Tutsi were racially superior and the Hutu were racially inferior . . . became an accepted 'scientific' truth during colonial

---

42. Sinema, *Who Must Die*, 73.
43. Straus, *Order of Genocide*, 20.
44. Straus, *Order of Genocide*, 225.

times."[45] The many well-documented accounts of the slaughter make very difficult reading.[46]

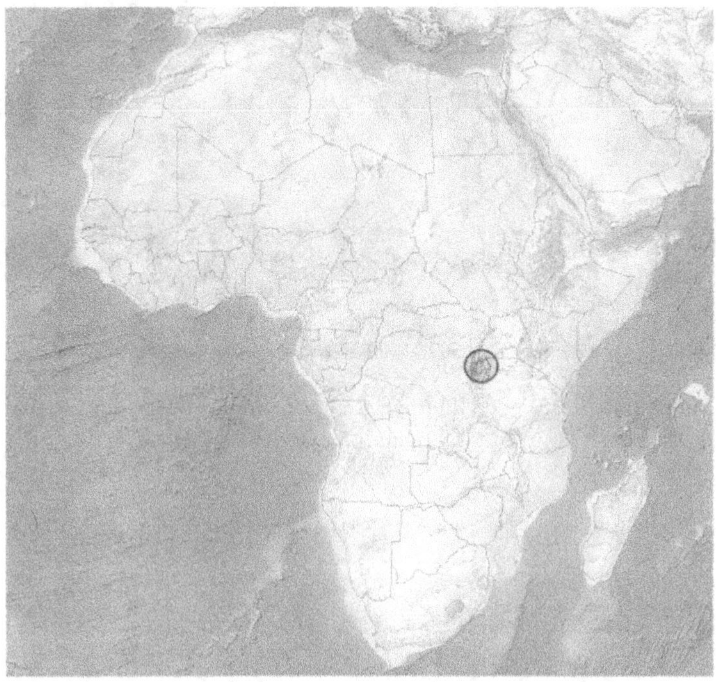

The location of the tiny country of Rwanda in south central Africa.[47]

45. Prunier, *Rwanda Crisis*, 11.

46. For example, see Jones, *Genocide*, 230–42.

47. From Wikimedia Commons: https://upload.wikimedia.org/wikipedia/commons/thumb/c/c4/Rwanda_in_Africa_%28relief%29_%28-mini_map%29.svg/640px-Rwanda_in_Africa_%28relief%29_%28-mini_map%29.svg.png.

A nurse attendant and children with severe hunger edema during the Biafra war at a Nigerian orphanage in the late 1960s.[48]

48. By CDC/Dr. Lyle Conrad, Sept. 26, 2006, from Wikimedia Commons: https://commons.wikimedia.org/wiki/File:Kwashiorkor_6903.jpg.

5

How Darwinism Birthed
Genocide in Nigeria

DARWINISM PLAYED A MAJOR role in the inhumane treatment and genocide of the native African population in Nigeria. The bias created by Darwinism in time moved to committing genocide in Africa.[1] Social Darwinism also justified the major economic exploitation of the African people by the British Empire and the British people. British rule of the Nigerian colony was a very dark period in world history that has left major negative effects even today on the Nigerians. The British Crown Colony government included much of West Africa, which eventually came to be known as Nigeria. Nigeria is Africa's most populous country, home to close to 20 percent of the entire sub-Saharan African population. It is Africa's largest producer of oil and natural gas and the world's eighth-largest oil producer. It is also currently blessed with Africa's largest economy.

Nigeria was ruled by the British Empire from the 1850s until October 1960, when the country finally achieved its independence. Britain's involvement was originally limited to charter companies

1. Wamwere, *Negative Ethnicity*.

and self-governing colonial administrators.[2] The British influence in Nigeria gradually increased during the nineteenth century until they occupied the entire area by 1885. Colonial expansion was driven largely by commercial interests dominated by "thorough going racism, justified by 'science' as Charles Darwin's views on natural selection were bowdlerized into 'social Darwinism.'"[3] History Professor William Cohen, in his chapter titled "Darwinism and Racism," observed that the "introduction of Darwinist thought [into Nigeria] reinforced the doctrine of racial inequality," which dominated the White colonizers of Africa, including in Nigeria.[4]

The fact is that, from day one, "British colonial rule was founded on the ideology that Africans, as a race, were inferior to Europeans."[5] Consequently, exploitation of the "inferior" native Africans by the "superior" race was seen as natural and appropriate. For example, before the colonial administration, residential segregation in Nigeria based on race, ethnicity, or religious lines did not exist.[6] Following their military conquest, the British imposed an economic system on the country designed to exploit African labor for profit. The administration and military control of the territory was handled primarily by White Britons, both those living in London and in Nigeria.

The belief in an "inferior race" was sometimes expressed in a very patronizing, demeaning way. For example, British politician and author Charles Sydney Goldman advised the "superior race" not to overlook the need to help "the inferior races."[7] Nonetheless, the idea that "the duty of the superior race is to aid the inferior in the course of its evolution" was often ignored.[8] The African hierarchies are well known and were often well respected by the British:

2. Moses, *Empire, Colony, Genocide*, 186.

3. Campbell and Page, *Nigeria*, 25.

4. Cohen, *French Encounter with Africans*, 248.

5. Falola and Heaton, *History of Nigeria*, 182.

6. Muhammad et al., "Review of Residential Segregation."

7. Goldman, *Empire and the Century*, 543.

8. Goldman, *Empire and the Century*, 542.

> The presence of a large black population results in the whole of the manual labor in which mere muscular energy counts, being performed by the inferior race, [and] white men occupying positions as overseers and skilled artisans.[9]

The British eventually, through a progressive sequence of regimes, imposed a form of rule on the Nigerian people that was both autocratic and bureaucratic. The result was that the policy of segregation was the most resented feature of colonial rule. Furthermore, the African natives disapproved of the large percentage of their tax money that was going to provide reservations and expensive bungalows for the privileged Europeans. They also resented "the removal of well-to-do Africans from their large homes, and the absolute neglect of the local towns" where the native Africans lived.[10]

THE ROLE OF CHRISTIAN MISSIONARIES

Christian missionaries gained influence throughout the 1800s, producing major positive transformations in the traditional African society.[11] Their positive influence included the erosion of the religious institutions that practiced human sacrifice and infanticide. Corrupt secret societies that had formerly played a major role in Nigerian political authority and community life also diminished.[12] Unfortunately, the church did far too little, too late to significantly help the native African people in Nigeria escape from the tyranny they suffered under the social Darwinism-inspired policies in Nigeria.

9. Goldman, *Empire and the Century*, 595.

10. Muhammad, "Review of Residential Segregation," 377.

11. Kolapo, *Christian Missionary Engagement*.

12. Kolapo, *Christian Missionary Engagement*, 90–96.

DARWINISM CRITICAL IN ENCOURAGING RACE HATRED

Long before British colonial rule was established in Africa, the intellectual climate in Western anthropology during the mid-nineteenth century influenced the relationship between British personnel and all indigenous peoples. This period was dominated by radical deterministic theories that were anchored in the belief that non-White peoples were biologically and culturally inferior to the White Caucasians. These racist ideas were intricately inter-twined with the academic field of anthropology in its formative years. Furthermore, "proponents of race theory in the nineteenth and early twentieth centuries liked to use the language of science to justify the most outrageous slaughters" and general mistreat-ment of native peoples.[13] A summary of the tragic influence of Darwinian beliefs in Africa by historian Zachary Liston accurately described the problem. These policies were developed in Europe and the US based on the idea

> that Darwin's ideas of survival of the fittest and natural selection applied to both race and ethnicity. Clearly these thoughts were . . . manipulated views of his teachings translated into different social realms to abuse power and influence. . . . Social Darwinism was a large influencer for the Nazi Germany regime and their imperialistic ef-forts. This was becoming a common tendency for many European nations and the U.S. at the turn of the century, as their imperialistic pursuits and goals continued to grow.[14]

Furthermore,

> the white races had claimed territory across the globe by right of strength and conquest. They had triumphed everywhere because they were the fittest; their triumphs were the proof of their fitness. Whole races had been an-nihilated . . . [that] were judged to have been unfit for life

13. Moses, *Empire, Colony, Genocide*, 164.
14. Liston, "Basis of Social Darwinism," para. 1.

> by the very fact that they had been exterminated. Living peoples across the world were categorized as "doomed" races. The only responsibility science had to such races was to record their cultures and collect artifacts from them, before their inevitable extinction. . . . Alongside the clearing of land, the coming of the railroad, and the settlement of white farmers, the eradication of indigenous tribes became a symbol of modernity. Social Darwinism thus cast itself as an agent of progress.[15]

Darwinian ideology aided in adversely damaging African-American rights and, as a result of racism, brought much social unrest to Nigeria. Social Darwinism was exploited to suppress large numbers of people who were judged as "inferior people."[16]

The end result of the mistreatment of the native people fulfilled the expectation of the German anthropologists who

> had been proclaiming the inevitable disappearance of the backward races since at least 1870, when the Darwinian, Oscar Peschel, editor of *Das Ausland*, wrote, "Everything that we acknowledge as the right of the individual will have to yield to the urgent demands of the [White] human society."[17]

The racism that emanated from the authorities in Britain was given official approval by the British government, which had a strong influence on the merchants, colonial administrators, and even the missionaries that immigrated into Africa from the 1860s until after 1900. The British did not hold a monopoly on these Darwinian views, as their equivalent existed in Germany, France, and other parts of mainland Europe.[18]

Under the commanding influence of Herbert Spencer and Charles Darwin, history was "biologized," thereby furnishing the basis for racism in Nigeria. Colonizers did not need to look very far to find justification for the ruthless exploitation of the African

---

15. Olusoga and Erichsen, *Kaiser's Holocaust*, 73.

16. Marney, *Structures of Prejudice*, 137.

17. Moses, *Empire, Colony, Genocide*, 172.

18. Cohen, *French Encounter with Africans*.

people in Nigeria. In Darwin's book, *The Descent of Man*, a chapter on "The Extinction of the Races of Man" was

> widely used in the mid-nineteenth [century] to justify the "disappearance" of "primitive races" on evolutionary grounds . . . the inferior organization makes room for the superior. As the Indian is killed by the approach of civilization, to which he resists in vain, so the black man perishes by that culture.[19]

Some of the claimed primitive traits of Black Africans based on the Darwinian worldview were described by historian Frederick Lugard, who concluded that the

> typical African . . . is a happy, thriftless, excitable person, lacking in self-control, discipline, and foresight, naturally courageous, and naturally courteous and polite, full of personal vanity, with littler sense of veracity, fond of music, and "loving weapons as an oriental loved jewelry . . . his mind . . . is *far nearer to the animal world than of the Europeans or Asiatic, and exhibits something of the animal's placidity*."[20]

Furthermore, he believed that Black Africans were culturally less evolved than the Europeans, and that the Black African race illustrated that "every stage in the evolution of human society . . . and every phase of human evolution may be studied as a living force."[21] To help control Black Africans as slaves, the following advice was given:

> The African negro is not naturally cruel, though his own insensibility to pain and his disregard for life—whether his own or another's—cause him to appear callous to suffering. . . . If mutilation and other inhuman punishment are inflicted, it is because nothing less would be a deterrent.[22]

19. Moses, *Empire, Colony, Genocide*, 164.
20. Lugard, *Dual Mandate*, 69. Emphasis added.
21. Lugard, *Dual Mandate*, 72, 75.
22. Lugard, *Dual Mandate*, 69.

Nevertheless, Lugard claimed that Blacks had, compared to Whites, a "more highly-developed brain and nervous system [which] increases the sensibility to physical pain."[23] Lugard asserts, "Evolution and progress are a law of nature," and for this reason, Whites have decisive "power over inferior races."[24] He also discusses in detail "primitive tribes" and their lower "stage of evolution."[25]

Furthermore, a comparative study of craniology by evolutionists had concluded that "neither Indians nor Africans had the brain power to become civilized."[26] From these comparisons came the conclusion by several leading scientists that they "were not interested in attempting to preserve primitive races," although they were "very interested in preserving slavery."[27]

PROHIBITING INTERMARRIAGE BETWEEN "SUPERIOR" AND "INFERIOR" RACES

Social Darwinists who supported racism in Nigeria also prohibited intermarriage between persons deemed "superior" with persons deemed to be a member of an "inferior" race. This prohibition was primarily between White and Black Africans, a prohibition enforced by miscegenation laws.

> [The] pattern that existed in pre-colonial Nigerian cities was altered by the advent of British colonialism. Prior to that time, there was a form of cohabitation among people of various national, social, and ethnic origins. However, the British resolved to put an end to this residential pattern. Spatial, legal, and psychological boundaries between social, ethnic, or racial categories were imposed to enforce a clear division between so-called races and

23. Lugard, *Dual Mandate*, 91.

24. Lugard, *Dual Mandate*, 132.

25. Lugard, *Dual Mandate*, 249.

26. Brantlinger, *Dark Vanishings*, 37.

27. Brantlinger, *Dark Vanishings*, 37.

ethnic groups to make these categories visible in every-day life.[28]

The reasoning used to justify such laws was that the White race was "the most advanced form of humanity, and had to be protected and fostered, while degenerate"[29] humans must eventually be exterminated for the good of all humanity. The Aryan race was considered to be highly evolved, whereas the "inferior" populations, such as African Blacks, were less evolved.[30] These beliefs, which were once widely accepted by leading American and British scientists,

> were hardly outside the pale. The existence of different human races, the superiority of the White race, and the need to protect and cultivate this superior race were widely held beliefs among most Western elites. Scholars in the most prestigious Western universities including Harvard, using orthodox science methods of the day, published studies that allegedly proved that members of the White race were more intelligent, more ethical, and more skilled than Africans or Indians.[31]

In addition, by "following the logic of Darwinian evolution, they argued that natural selection must be allowed to weed out unfit individuals and leave only the fittest to survive" and reproduce their kind to build a superior race in the future.[32]

Regarded as the highest-evolved race, the "Aryan race had the finest qualities—rationalism, beauty, integrity, diligence. The Aryan race had the potential to turn man into superman."[33] If other races were allowed to "intermarry with Aryans, they would adulterate all human populations and doom *Homo sapiens* to

28. Harari, *Sapiens*, 232.

29. Harari, *Sapiens*, 232.

30. Harari, *Sapiens*, 232.

31. Harari, *Sapiens*, 232–33.

32. Harari, *Sapiens*, 233.

33. Harari, *Sapiens*, 232.

extinction."[34] Therefore, the more committed Darwin supporters argued that the strict social Darwinian mindset taught that the *inferior races* must be extinguished at all costs. These racial doctrines contributed to the rise of the African separatist churches in Nigeria that for decades had operated under British rule. In the administrative sector, this doctrine enforced residential segregation for much of British rule in their colonies.[35]

Besides the evolutionary hierarchy between Whites and Blacks enacted upon the arrival of white colonization, "the purer black races had [already] established their domination over the inferior [race], and ruled by force of superior intelligence and cultivation long before that time."[36] Furthermore, in judging the African people, one must evaluate "the stage of human evolution when sedentary habits replaced nomadic tendencies."[37] Also, while not an issue when Whites enslaved Africans, slavery where the "owner is in the same stage of evolution as the slave," was a concern when Africans enslaved Africans.

THE SEVERITY OF THE PROBLEMS
CAUSED BY SOCIAL DARWINISM

Social Darwinism is "as dangerous as a tiger. . . . [And] a large portion of Northern Nigeria's suffering can be laid directly at the feet of a tiger and its parent."[38] This "tiger" has led to many of the problems that still exist today in Nigeria. For example,

> residential segregation in Nigeria was reviewed from the pre-colonial, colonial, to the post-colonial era, and finally the consequences of residential segregation . . . has revealed that prior to the British colonial rule there existed no residential differentiation based on ethnicity or race, people of diverse tribes and nationalities cohabited

34. Harari, *Sapiens*, 232.

35. Alozie, "Space and Colonial Alterity," 5.

36. Lugard, *Dual Mandate*, 76.

37. Lugard, *Dual Mandate*, 355.

38. Oluniyi, "Cruel Legacy of Social Darwinism," para. 2.

in the north. The creation of residential segregation by the colonial administrators . . . has led to the present inaccessibility of the poor to affordable housing, security, inadequate provision of infrastructure in the high-density residential areas, and most importantly the cause of ethno-religious conflicts in [and] across Nigeria.[39]

The iron rule in Nigeria was enforced by the forty-five thousand soldiers who served in the British Armed Forces in Africa and Southeast Asia. The Nigerian regiments formed the majority of the 81st and 82nd West African Divisions of the British Army. In short,

> Darwin's theory of evolution further posited the natural world as a place where the fittest survive and the less-fit decline and die; if this is indeed the case, thought Darwin's contemporaries (and indeed many of our own), then . . . Why should we not let the less-fit die? Indeed, why should we not hasten their demise if it will profit us—the survivors, the fittest—economically, geographically, or politically? Why should the Briton not manipulate, oppress, and exploit the Nigerian? After all, the fact that he can do so surely proves that he is right to do so—he is fulfilling his very destiny, as decreed by Nature herself.[40]

RACIAL INFERIORITY IDEAS
EXISTED BEFORE DARWIN

The book, *Essay on the Inequality of the Human Races, 1853–1855*, authored by French aristocrat, novelist, author, diplomat, and traveler Arthur de Gobineau, made an important early contribution to the racist Darwinian movement.[41] Gobineau is best known today for helping to introduce into society the "scientific" race theory that was used in developing the "master race" belief. Gobineau

39. Muhammad, "Review of Residential Segregation," 382.
40. Oluniyi, "Cruel Legacy of Social Darwinism," para. 6.
41. Goineau, *Essay on the Inequality*.

argued that aristocrats like himself were intellectually and otherwise superior to commoners. He also concluded that the reason for this was that aristocrats possessed more Aryan genetic traits than commoners due to less interbreeding with the inferior non-Aryan races.

Gobineau's best-selling book argued,

> The Negro people belong to a separate race of mankind. The Negro race has an entirely different ancestry [than the Whites]. . . . The Negro race has a place in the biological hierarchy somewhere between the white man and the anthropoids.[42]

Furthermore, Gobineau added, the "Negro" must be kept in his "inferior place" to prevent deterioration of the "superior race."[43] Gobineau's basic conclusion was in

> the superiority of the white race over others . . . labeled the "Aryans," i.e., the Germanic peoples—as representing the summit of civilization. He advanced the theory that the fate of civilizations is determined by racial composition, that white and in particular Aryan societies flourish as long as they remain free of black and yellow strains, and that the more a civilization's racial character is diluted through miscegenation, the more likely it is to lose its vitality and creativity and sink into corruption and immorality.[44]

Although Gobineau's work "was virtually ignored" at first and appealed to only a "handful of reactionary aesthetes," it took off when Darwin entered the world of evolutionary science. Once Darwin's work was widely accepted, Gobineau's "theory of racial determinism had an 'enormous' influence upon the subsequent development of racist theories and practices in Western Europe."[45]

42. Marney, *Structures of Prejudice*, 137.
43. Marney, *Structures of Prejudice*, 137.
44. *Encyclopaedia Britannica Online*, "Arthur de Gobineau."
45. *Encyclopaedia Britannica Online*, "Arthur de Gobineau."

At this time, before Darwin, there were other early evolutionists, such as the German scholar Johann Blumenbach, who, in his book *On the Natural Variety of Mankind*, identified five different races based on his study of sixty different skulls. Blumenbach argued that all humans derived from a single origin and that environmental factors degenerated the human stock, resulting in the five races that he identified.[46]

POLYGENESIS THEORY VS. MONOGENESIS THEORY

The polygenesis theory (that all the races evolved separately) and the monogenesis theory (that all races had a common ancestor, such as Adam) were fiercely contested for decades.[47] Most evolutionists preferred polygenesis and, in contrast, "Christian leaders favored monogenesis based on a biblical understanding of Adam and Eve as the common progenitors of all humanity."[48] Although he himself was a monogenist, Darwin's work "enjoyed massive success" and produced wide acceptance of the polygenesis view that shaped "early colonial perceptions of Africans as racially inferior" to the Europeans.[49] This polygenesis theory, that all humans evolved from different prehuman species, was commonly used to justify the mistreatment of Africans.[50] This view held sway until after WWII and the Holocaust, which forced scientists to accept the monogenesis view.[51]

46. Blumenbach, *On the Natural Variety*.

47. Decker and McMahon, *Idea of Development in Africa*, 61.

48. Decker and McMahon, *Idea of Development in Africa*, 61.

49. Decker and McMahon, *Idea of Development in Africa*, 61.

50. Decker and McMahon, *Idea of Development in Africa*, 62.

51. Glick, *Comparative Reception of Darwinism*, 162.

SUMMARY

The rejection of the belief that all men are descended from one couple, Adam and Eve, and its replacement by Darwinism, had a major influence on the racism and genocide that occurred during the last century. In many African countries, in time, they moved "from bias to Genocide."[52] If the creation view had been firmly held and accepted by the peoples of the earth, the outcome of the last century would have been very different. The example of Nigeria is only one of many revealing the harm caused by social Darwinism.

**Prisoners from the Herero and Nama tribes
during the 1904–1908 war against Germany.**[53]

52. Wamwere, *Negative Ethnicity*'s subtitle: *From Bias to Genocide*.

53. From Wikimedia Commons: https://commons.wikimedia.org/wiki/File:Herero_and_Nama_prisoners.jpg.

6

The Central Role of Darwinism in the Herero and Namibian Genocides

THE HERERO AND NAMIBIAN 1904–1907 genocides of those living in German South West Africa cost the lives of over one hundred thousand native Africans.[1] This was among the many tragedies in Africa caused by the ideas propagated in Charles Darwin's writings. Furthermore, "Charles Darwin's scholarly circle grew immeasurable over the 1860s, encircling the entire Western world," including, especially, Germany.[2] Darwin specifically discussed the evolutionary clash of advanced (meaning "more evolved") humans and primitive (meaning "less evolved") humans. This is exactly what happened when the Germans endeavored to steal the land and minerals of the Herero and Namibian people. In the end, the clash resulted in the brutal genocide of most of the Herero and Namibian people. This genocide was couched in overtly Darwinian terms in an attempt to justify its chief protagonists.[3]

1. Sarkin, *Colonial Genocide and Reparations Claims.*

2. Kendi, *Stamped from the Beginning,* 210.

3. Olusoga and Erichsen, *Kaiser's Holocaust,* 294.

THE GENOCIDE OF THE HERERO AND NAMIBIAN PEOPLE

The Nazi racial policies that led to the concentration camps and the mass genocide of "inferior, less evolved" people during World War II, resulted in the murder of over fifty-five million persons. These crimes were a product of the minds of several leading German academics. However, the seeds of genocide were not born in the 1930s with Hitler's rule, as commonly believed. Rather, they were born during the nineteenth century in Africa, towards the end of the 1890s by German social Darwinists.[4] The connection between Darwin and the exploitation of native Africans was explained by Oluniyi:

> Darwin's theory of evolution . . . posited the natural world as a place where the fittest survive and the less-fit decline and die; if this is indeed the case, thought Darwin's contemporaries (and indeed many of our own), then who are we to battle nature herself? Why should we not let the less-fit die? Indeed, why should we not hasten their demise if it will profit us—the survivors, the fittest—economically, geographically, and politically? Why should the Briton not manipulate, oppress, and exploit the Nigerian? After all, the fact that he can do so surely proves that he is *right* to do so—he is fulfilling his very destiny, as decreed by Nature herself.[5]

Darwin's own words accurately described the African situation and imply approval of what happened in Africa when the Europeans confronted the native African peoples:

> Extinction follows chiefly from competition of tribe with tribe, and race with race . . . when one of two adjoining tribes becomes more numerous and powerful than the other, the contest is soon settled by war, slaughter, cannibalism, slavery, and absorption. Even when a weaker tribe is not thus abruptly swept away, if it once begins to decrease, it generally goes on decreasing until it is

4. Olusoga and Erichsen, *Kaiser's Holocaust*.
5. Oluniyi, *Darwin Comes to Africa*, 16. Emphasis in original.

> extinct. When civilized nations come into contact with
> barbarians the struggle is short . . . the causes which lead
> the victory of civilized nations . . . will be fatal in many
> ways to savages.[6]

During the colonial land grab of African countries by European nations after the 1884–1885 Berlin Conference, Germany was given the country of Namibia, then known as South West Africa. German settlers ran roughshod over the historical rights and claims of the Herero tribal inhabitants. For the next twenty years, they continued to plunder the native peoples' lands, houses, and livestock.

Based on what was judged to be the Herero's apelike appearance, they were commonly referred to by Germans as "baboons." This perception was taken as evidence of their less-evolved status compared to White Europeans. Many Herero men were beaten to death for minor infringements, and some of the young Herero women were forced to become sex slaves to serve both the German soldiers and settlers.[7]

The genocide of the Herero and Namibian peoples in German South West Africa was perpetrated by soldiers and bureaucrats who traveled from Kaiser Wilhelm's Germany to Africa with the blessing of German Chancellor Bismarck. After German settlers began to steal the indigenous peoples' property and livestock, the Herero and the Namibian people felt they had no choice but to attempt to resist. The German government retaliated to their attempts to resist by launching a war of extermination, in which Africans were forced to work to death or were outright murdered.[8]

German colonial authorities envisioned a predominantly White African Germany, wherein the native populations would be forced into reservations and their land distributed among the European settlers.[9] When the German colonists decided among themselves that they wanted the land and wealth of the native

6. Darwin, *Descent of Man*, 238.

7. Gewald, *Herero Heroes*.

8. Gewald, *Herero Heroes*.

9. Gewald, *Herero Heroes*.

Namibian people, they formally and aggressively began implementing their takeover. As expected, the Herero and Namibian peoples aggressively opposed the German plan. Consequently, on January 12, 1904, war began between the Germans and the Herero and Namibian peoples.

THE NAMIBIAN-GERMAN WAR BEGINS

When the Namibians strenuously resisted, Berlin's response to what they viewed as an insurrection was rapid and ruthless. Kaiser Wilhelm II dispatched fourteen thousand troops to what they called German East Africa (today's Rwanda, Burundi, and Tanzania) under the command of a ten-year veteran of the German colonial army, General Lieutenant-General Lothar von Trotha, who "believed in Darwin's 'superior race,' 'survival-of-the-fittest-through-"cleansing"-of-the-weakest' views."[10] Lothar von Trotha was renowned for the ruthless efficiency that he employed to suppress the 1900 China Boxer Rebellion. He likewise ruthlessly quashed the resistance of the Herero and Namibian people who opposed Germany's occupation of their land and property.

In 1904, von Trotha, convinced that all "Negroes" had the same low mentality level and would yield only to force, published an extermination order: "It was and remains my policy to apply this force by absolute terrorism and even cruelty. I shall destroy the . . . tribes by shedding rivers of blood and money."[11] The "aim of the war was annihilation of the whole lot" of Herero and Namibian "Negroes."[12] The German settlers "had an inborn feeling of belonging to a superior race," which they believed gave them the right to "shed rivers of blood and money" to achieve their goal.[13]

In the end, in response to the uprising by the Herero people against the German encroachment on their land, about 80 percent

10. Carroll, *Survivors*, 78.

11. Mentan, *Recurrent Genocidal Nightmares*, 212.

12. Olusoga and Erichsen, *Kaiser's Holocaust*, 142.

13. Totten and Hitchcock, *Genocide of Indigenous Peoples*, 127.

of the nation's native people were systematically killed through battle, deliberate starvation and thirst, as well as being worked to death in barbaric German death camps. The so-called "war" involved trained German soldiers using powerful guns and cannons against the Herero people, who were armed with nothing but knives and fright when they saw what was happening to their families and people. A handful of German soldiers were killed compared to thousands of Herero tribesmen. Social Darwinism gave militarists and racists the "scientific" authority to "explain away terrible acts and justify the destruction or enslavement of other peoples as being natural, inevitable, and therefore somehow moral."[14]

The German records described the genocide as defeating the Herero tribe (of Southern and South West Africa) in the Battle of Waterberg. In his infamous Vernichtungsbefehl (annihilation order), von Trotha stated in the 1904 campaign order, "Every Herero, with or without a gun, with or without cattle, will be shot. I will no longer . . . [exempt] women and children, I will drive them back to their people or I will let them be shot."[15]

The details illustrate the brutality of the massacre and how the remaining Herero were driven into the Kalahari Desert, where most died a horrible death of dehydration:

> In a decisive battle at Hamakari, near Waterberg, on 11 August 1904, von Trotha's troops surrounded the Herero tribes people on three sides and brutally defeated them. In a cynical ploy, he left open only the way into the Omaheke area of the Kalahari Desert. The battle plan was that those who escaped the German bullets should die of thirst. Waterholes for 150 miles (240 km) around the desert were either patrolled or poisoned, and those Herero who came crawling out of the Omaheke, desperate for water, were bayoneted.[16]

14. Olusoga and Erichsen, *Kaiser's Holocaust*, 294.

15. Bartrop, *Encountering Genocide*, 11.

16. Ambler, "Herero Genocide," 53.

For three years, many of the surviving Herero and Namibians were interned in a concentration camp on Shark Island, where conscious neglect led to a horrific death toll. An enormous graveyard on the outskirts of the Namibian seaside resort of Swakopmund contains the bones of many of those murdered in the late 1800s in German concentration camps. Roughly half of the total surviving Herero and Namibian populations, about seventy-five thousand men and women, perished in an event that historians today consider the first mass genocide of the nineteenth and twentieth centuries.[17] The perpetrators of this genocide justified their actions by invoking conclusions based firmly on social Darwinian evolution that the fate of the so-called dark races of the world was

> governed by the same laws of natural selection. Surely, their disappearance was a result of their inability to adapt to the arrival of stronger, more capable races and the civilization they brought with them? The annihilation of the Tasmanians, the Patagonians, the Native Americans, and perhaps soon the Africans all testified to their innate weakness, their unfitness for the future.[18]

Historians have estimated that, all total, between twenty-four thousand and one hundred thousand Hereros and approximately ten thousand Namibians were killed. The Herero and Namibian massacres have been correctly identified as a genocide because Lothar von Trotha was instructed not to harm Englishmen, missionaries, and people of other tribes. Only the Herero and Namibian people were to be murdered. Professors Olusoga and Erichsen state that when Africa became the focus for new colonial conquests in the latter half of the century,

> the destruction of indigenous peoples was increasingly explained using ideas drawn from science rather than scripture. While the advent of Darwinism represented a direct and powerful challenge to the Church, the religious scandal surrounding the publication of *On the Origin of Species* has tended to obscure the fact that, in many

17. Gewald, *Herero Heroes.*

18. Olusoga and Erichsen, *Kaiser's Holocaust*, 72.

ways, Darwin's ideas were perfectly in keeping with his times. While the religious establishment was rocked to its foundations, much of the Victorian scientific elite, along with various economists, philosophers, and politicians, welcomed 'Darwinism' wholeheartedly.[19]

The result was a Darwinian theory that advanced concepts allowing the Germans to thrust wide open the doors that German scientists had unlocked.[20] The German governor, Theodor Leutwein, admitted that the German settlers' "inborn feeling of belonging to a superior race" resulted in horrible mistreatment of the native people.[21]

THE INFLUENCE OF SOCIAL DARWINISM

The popularity of Charles Darwin's writings occurred at about the same time when Europe was looking for an excuse to exploit the enormous wealth of Africa.[22] Although

> Germany's scientists stood at the forefront of the Darwinian revolution, in her African empire . . . her colonialists were confronted with a situation that was at odds with the fundamental racial suppositions at the heart of imperialism. Germany's only African colony suitable for large-scale white settlement remained dominated by tribes of Africans. . . . The Nama and Herero had not retreated into the hinterland in the face of the white man, nor had they fallen prey to introduced disease.[23]

The Herero genocide was largely ignored by most nations of the world. As explained by Lindqvist, it was because "the great

---

19. Olusoga and Erichsen, *Kaiser's Holocaust*, 72.

20. McGregor, "German and American Eugenics."

21. Gewald, *Herero Heroes*, 145.

22. Oluniyi, *Darwin Comes to Africa*, 17.

23. Olusoga and Erichsen, *Kaiser's Holocaust*, 75.

powers had little desire to interfere with . . . genocide, for they themselves had similar skeletons in their cupboards."[24]

Ian Thompson documented that it was "the social Darwinists and eugenicists in late-nineteenth-century Germany who helped to create new values of totalitarian dominance" in Nazi Germany.[25] Furthermore, he added that

> Darwin's *On the Origin of Species*, with its brutally materialist account of nature as bleak survivalism, was made to serve as justification for the extermination of Namibian tribes and, later, for Hitler's biological anti-Semitism. In a racist age, nature was seen as a competitive marketplace, where black people were born to be mastered, and the fittest survived.[26]

As Thompson documented, the Darwinian influence on the genocidal racism of Africa was obvious:

> Armed with callipers and craniometry charts, the Kaiser's race engineers were keen to measure the severed heads of Nama tribesmen: handle-shaped ears, prehensile feet and other "apish" stigmata were considered telltale atavisms. Civilization, according to these pseudo-scientists, depended on the separation of races, not on their harmonious integration.[27]

Furthermore, eugenic studies inspired by "a powerful idea"—Darwinism—created "a social myth" that spread throughout the Western world.[28] The leading American monograph on eugenics, *The Kallikak Family* by Henry Goddard,[29] was translated into German in 1914. The full text appeared in the German academic journal *Friedrich Mann's Pedagogishes Magazin*. As a result, this American eugenic study had a significant impact on Nazi

---

24. Lindqvist, *Exterminate All the Brutes*, 27.

25. Lindqvist, *Exterminate All the Brutes*, 27.

26. Thompson, "Kaiser's Holocaust," para. 8.

27. Thompson, "Kaiser's Holocaust," para. 8.

28. Smith, *Minds Made Feeble*, 193.

29. Goddard, *Kallikak Family*.

Germany's racist policies that resulting in the Holocaust. The fact is that science has lent much prestige to both social Darwinist thought and the notion of scientific racism. In short, racism had the imprimatur of science, which provided the justification for the belief that the "more evolved race" had the right to rule other races, all of which undergirded imperialist domination of non-Western peoples.

After the war, the few surviving Herero natives over the age of seven were required to wear a metal disc around their necks with their registration number that designated them as free labor.[30] Similarly, in the Jewish/Slavic Holocaust, Hitler required Jews to wear a Star of David and enslaved those persons he considered to be part of an inferior race.

WHY GERMANY SUPPORTED SOCIAL DARWINISM

One major reason Germany was very receptive to the theory of evolution was because it was supported by many prominent American and British scientists. Furthermore,

> Germany was particularly receptive to Darwin, partly because his ideas attracted the support of a number of well-respected German scientists. Chief among them was Ernst Haeckel, one of Germany's most esteemed intellectuals. Haeckel began to explore what very quickly became known as Darwinism soon after the publication of *On the Origin of Species*. Over the next forty years, he wrote a stream of highly influential books on evolution, some of which became among the most popular works of non-fiction published in Germany during the age of the Kaisers. A generation of German scientists and intellectuals came to know Darwin partly through the filter of Ernst Haeckel, and one of the key characteristics of Haeckel's work was the way in which he applied Darwin's theories to human racial difference.[31]

30. Gewald, *Herero Heroes*, 145.

31. Olusoga and Erichsen, *Kaiser's Holocaust*, 75.

THE INFLUENCE OF HAECKEL

The callous attitude toward the native people, who were judged as "inferior beings," was a product of Darwinism that, in Germany, was actively promoted by Darwin's leading German disciple, Ernst Haeckel:

> That the German settlers and a high-ranking officer like General von Trotha would hold to these "superior race," "survival-of-the-fittest-through-'cleansing'-of-the-weakest" views are hardly surprising. Darwin's *On the Origin of Species* (which is subtitled *by Means of Natural Selection or the Preservation of Favored Races in the Struggle for Life*) had been translated into German in 1875, and his evolutionary theories had for decades been avidly promoted to all and sundry by the popular books and theatrical presentations of Ernst Haeckel ["Darwin's Bulldog on the Continent"].[32]

Haeckel went well beyond Darwin to justify the subjugation of not only the African races but also the people of other nations that the evolutionary scientists of his day regarded as evolutionarily inferior humans. The German march to further human evolution by eugenics was seen as essential in colonizing those Africans that they regarded as subhumans.

OVERCROWDING CONCERNS IN GERMANY

In the last quarter of the nineteenth century, Germany experienced a baby boom, resulting in the overcrowding of many German cities. Emigration was one solution, as was Lebensraum, the Darwinian doctrine that justified taking land belonging to those the eugenists regarded as inferior peoples. Emigration allowed the self-designated "superior race," German Aryans, to increase. The Germans believed that they had to ensure that their Aryan German communities grew and prospered by any means necessary. In their minds, this belief justified the racial Völkisch theory that

32. Ambler, "Herero Genocide," 53.

was eventually to be implemented in both German colonies and in Nazi Germany itself. Although German

> imperialism could be justified by a number of arguments—economic self-interest, European rivalry, and the white man's duty to spread civilization and the Gospels—the extermination of whole races was more difficult to explain. Yet Social Darwinism, along with a range of racial theories taken from the older Scientific Racism of the late eighteenth and early nineteenth centuries, was able to recast both historical and contemporary events, and in this capacity, it took on the twisted logic of a witch trial.[33]

The result was that the Whites, based on Darwinism, "had claimed territory across the globe by right of strength and conquest."[34] They reasoned that they, the Germans,

> were the fittest; their triumphs were the proof of their fitness. Whole races, who had been annihilated long before Darwin had put pen to paper, were judged to have been unfit for life by the very fact that they had been exterminated. Living people across the world were categorized as "doomed races." The only responsibility science had to such races was to record their cultures and collect artifacts from them, before their inevitable extinction.[35]

Due to the influence of Darwinism, the

> spread of Europeans across the globe came to be regarded as an almost sacred enterprise and was increasingly linked to that other holy crusade of the nineteenth century—the march of progress. Alongside the clearing of land, the coming of the railways and the settlement of white farmers, the eradication of indigenous tribes became a symbol of modernity. Social Darwinism thus cast death itself as an agent of progress. The notion that the strong were destined to overcome the weak in the

33. Olusoga and Erichsen, *Kaiser's Holocaust*, 72.

34. Olusoga and Erichsen, *Kaiser's Holocaust*, 72–73.

35. Olusoga and Erichsen, *Kaiser's Holocaust*, 73.

struggle for life became almost a mantra, repeated thousands of times in memoirs, speeches, biographies, and scientific tracts.[36]

Any last remnants of Christian morality or guilt could be allayed by the fact that the demise of the native Africans was, as proven by Darwin's own words, inevitable:

> When civilized nations come into contact with barbarians the struggle is short. . . . Of the causes which lead to the victory of civilized nations, some are plain and simple, others complex and obscure. We can see that the cultivation of the land will be fatal in many ways to savages, for they cannot, or will not, change their habits.[37]

The main person who implemented the African holocaust was the general mentioned above, Lothar von Trotha. Between 1894 and 1897, von Trotha's aides executed thousands of Herero and Namibian people.[38] They used every possible brutal means to achieve their genocidal goal. In 1908, General von Trotha was replaced by Friedrich von Lindequist, who continued the inhumane programs begun by his predecessor. From 1908 to 1913, Lindequist enriched Germany by fifty-two million marks worth of diamonds mined in Africa, which they later used to fund the wars in Europe. In addition, thousands of Africans were literally worked to death digging for gold in the scorching desert sands near cities and settlements.[39]

Eventually, as a result of missionary pressure and the growing labor shortage in the colony, von Trotha's extermination campaign was eventually ended by Berlin. The surviving Herero people were placed in concentration camps where they were forced into "slave labor, overworked, hungry, and exposed to diseases such as typhoid and smallpox."[40]

---

36. Olusoga and Erichsen, *Kaiser's Holocaust*, 73–74.

37. Darwin, *Descent of Man*, 2nd ed., 182.

38. Olusoga and Erichsen, *Kaiser's Holocaust*, 150.

39. Olusoga and Erichsen, *Kaiser's Holocaust*.

40. Mamdani, *When Victims Become Killers*, 12.

THE CONCENTRATION CAMPS

Africa's five main German-built concentration camps were all located in what is Namibia today. About this time, Africa became the field laboratory for German racial scientists to study the remaining "inferior races" still living there. To obtain evidence to support human evolution, female prisoners in one concentration camp

> were forced to boil the severed heads of their own people and scrape the flesh, sinews, and ligaments off of the skull with shards of broken glass. . . . The skulls were then placed into crates by the German soldiers and shipped to museums, collections, and universities in Germany.[41]

One Berlin University scientist, ironically named Christian Fetzer, used the skulls in an attempt to prove human evolution by pointing out what he claimed were the similarities between the Nama people and the anthropoid apes.[42]

INTERRACIAL MARRIAGE CONDEMNED

The fear of racial degeneration as a result of racial mixture prompted the German scientific establishment to warn against interracial marriage with racially inferior persons. It was actually "illegal for white people to have sex with people defined as having a different skin color."[43] One of the most well-known pioneers in the scientific racial field was Berlin University professor Eugene Fischer. His seminal book on race, written with professors Erwin Baur and Fritz Lenz, was so valued by Hitler that it was placed in a prominent place on Hitler's study table. Fischer warned in this book against Aryans intermixing with inferior races, especially the African Negroes. This view was supported by law in the German government controlling Namibia.[44]

41. Olusoga and Erichsen, *Kaiser's Holocaust*, 224.
42. Olusoga and Erichsen, *Kaiser's Holocaust*, 225.
43. Carroll, *Survivors*, 78.
44. Gewald, *Herero Heroes*.

Although Germany became involved in the colonial movement much later than Spain, England, and Portugal, German

> scientists had been among the first to accept the logic of Social Darwinism. In 1868, while working on *The Descent of Man*, Darwin, in a letter to Wilhelm Preyer, Professor of Physiology at the University of Jena, reported that "The support I receive from Germany is my chief ground for hoping that our views [on race] will ultimately prevail."[45]

Many military veterans responsible for the German atrocities in Africa later joined the Nazi party and "soldiers and scientists whose careers began on the pastoral deserts of South West Africa, or on the killing fields of East Africa, Togo, and Cameroon were to play leading roles in the Nazi tragedy."[46]

Another famous German involved in the African holocaust was Hermann Göring's father, Dr. Heinrich Göring. He was appointed by the "Iron Chancellor" himself, Otto von Bismarck, to establish the German African colonies. To achieve this goal, new German towns were built, one of which was the African city of Luderitz. Another prominent man who supported the social Darwinian vision for Africa was British explorer William Winwood Reade. He captured the growing Darwinian consensus of his age in his book *Savage Africa*, which concluded with a prophecy of the continent's future founded on his "unshakeable belief that Africa belonged to the white man."[47] To achieve this goal, the "Negroes" would be required to work as slaves to convert Africa into a White man's paradise. When this goal was achieved, as an inferior race, the "Negroes" would eventually be exterminated. In Reade's words,

> Africa shall be redeemed. Her children shall perform this mighty work. Her morasses shall be drained; her deserts shall be watered by canals; her forests shall be reduced to firewood. Her children shall do all this. They shall pour an *elixir vitae* into the veins of their mother, now

45. Olusoga and Erichsen, *Kaiser's Holocaust*, 74.

46. Olusoga and Erichsen, *Kaiser's Holocaust*, 74.

47. Olusoga and Erichsen, *Kaiser's Holocaust*, 109.

withered and diseased. They shall restore her to youth and to immortal beauty. In this amenable task they may possibly become exterminated. We must learn to look at this result with composure. It illustrates the beneficent law of Nature, that the weak must be devoured by the strong.[48]

Reade also fervently believed that Europeans would in the not-too-distant future construct large estates in Africa owned by Germans. On these estates "young ladies on camp stools under palm trees will read with tears *The Last of the Negroes*, and the Niger will become as romantic a river as the Rhine."[49]

Some Germans advocated an unbridled form of colonialism to harness

> Ernest Haeckel, one of "Germany's most esteemed intellectuals [who accepted his own] . . . version of Social Darwinism in order to dismiss the views of the humanitarians as hopelessly outdated and unscientific. After all, there was no humanitarianism, compassion, or brotherhood in nature."[50]

Take, for example, German scientist Friedrich Ratzel, whose theories

> were heavily influenced by concepts drawn from his zoological background and the work of his original mentor, Ernst Haeckel. Ratzel's interest in the anatomical sciences remained strong for much of his life. One of his many friends, with whom he maintained a healthy correspondence, was the racial anthropologist Felix von Luschan.[51]

In the late 1890s, Ratzel began to fuse ideas inspired by social Darwinism with the

---

48. Reade, *Savage Africa*, 452.

49. Reade, *Savage Africa*, 452–53.

50. Olusoga and Erichsen, *Kaiser's Holocaust*, 74.

51. Olusoga and Erichsen, *Kaiser's Holocaust*, 109.

notion of the "struggle for existence" to the study of migration, both animal and human. To Ratzel, the invasion and colonization of the world outside Europe by the white race, and the displacement of indigenous peoples, was all part of the "struggle for existence," motivated above all by the search for "living space." Darwin had shown that when animals moved to new environments, over time they adapted and evolved to those new conditions. From this Ratzel concluded that when human races migrated they adapted their cultures to the new environment. If a race was successful in adapting to the conditions of a different territory, their culture advanced and their population increased.[52]

Furthermore, in Ratzel's view, human history was driven forward by a series of migrations, such as from Europe to Africa, that resulted in their adaptation to new environments. Ironically, evolutionary paleoanthropologists see this as a return to man's continent of origin—a return to our common evolutionary ancestors' roots in Africa. Each adaptation advanced the culture of the migrating race. Ratzel even speculated as to whether the drive to migrate was itself a main feature of a virile and vigorous race.

After World War I, although the British exposed many German crimes in Africa, the African genocide was ignored by many historians. This historical event documents the fact that the roots of the most infamous holocaust in modern history—the Jewish Holocaust—were first planted and implemented in Africa. The bestial dimensions of the human mind, driven by Darwinism, did not begin with Hitler. The fact is that almost from the first day that Francis Galton, the half-cousin of Charles Darwin, coined the word "eugenics," it has been connected with militarism.[53]

52. Olusoga and Erichsen, *Kaiser's Holocaust*, 109.
53. Kellogg, *Headquarter Nights*, 99–108.

SUMMARY

Unfortunately, "the critical link between the increasingly insatiable appetite for Africa's resources on one hand, and Charles Darwin's growing visibility on the other hand, has been ignored" by most leading references and the public media.[54] As this brief review has established, the well-documented evidence for the Darwinian harm in Africa is overwhelming. "Race branding" was based on evolutionary thinking caused by the "survival-of-the-fittest" doctrine.

The idea that different races are at different stages of evolution has produced, as its logical offspring, the murder of tens of millions of innocent mothers, fathers, sons, and daughters in the twentieth century, beginning with the Herero and Namibian genocide. The result of the genocide was that, from 1904 to 1908, the Herero were reduced from a tribe of over eighty thousand persons to about fifteen thousand often-starving refugees.[55]

Decades later, Hitler would proclaim the same Darwinist superiority views to justify the Nazi subjugation of the "lesser" races of Europe, the Jews and Slavic people. This would be one more example of the rotten fruit of "superior race," "survival-of-the-fittest-through-'cleansing'-of-the-weakest" views.[56]

54. Olusoga and Erichsen, *Kaiser's Holocaust*, 17.
55. *Encyclopaedia Britannica*, "Herero Genocide."
56. Olusoga and Erichsen, *Kaiser's Holocaust*, 74.

"Condition of Herero on surrender after having been driven into the desert."[57]

57. From Wikimedia Commons: https://commons.wikimedia.org/wiki/ File:Emaciated_Herero_upon_surrender.jpg.

7

The French African Colonies' Holocaust

INTRODUCTION

The adverse influence of Darwinism was felt in almost every African country, including the French colonies, which often resulted in grossly inhuman treatment of the native peoples. Professor Hamel correctly observed,

> Against the rising voice of the abolition movement, those who defended slavery insisted on the innate inferiority of black Africans, using . . . social Darwinism to justify the enslavement of blacks. This negative notion of race led to the legal segregation of races and racist policies.[1]

France colonized many African nations, primarily in North and West Africa, but also in East and Central Africa. The larger colonized areas include modern-day Algeria, Morocco, Tunisia, Mauritania, Mali, Niger, Chad, and parts of the Sahel region. Additionally, French colonial territories encompassed parts of West Africa, Equatorial Africa, and Madagascar. The fact is, in these territories,

---

1. Hamel, *Black Morocco*, 101.

throughout the 19th and first half of the 20th centuries, France systematically carried out policies of genocide and ethnic cleansing against the indigenous peoples of the countries it occupied. . . . Historically, France exterminated the peoples of Morocco, Tunisia, Algeria, [and] Djibouti.[2]

Darwinism greatly affected how the Europeans treated the native Africans in all of these colonial nations. Depending on the country and, most importantly, the European administration, the treatment of the native Africans by the French varied widely. Racial distinctions based on unchangeable physical differences varied, and until

the mid-twentieth century, people of European ancestry generally assumed that such racial demarcations reflected natural white superiority. The color line was seen as having been drawn by God or biology. . . . Slavery, proscriptions against miscegenation, colonialism, imperialism, manifest destiny, racially exclusive forms of citizenship or nationalism, and exploitation were justified by whites as preordained in nature.[3]

Professor Marx added that these assumptions of natural racial distinctions, were enforced by the Nazis and Europeans in general because this

discrimination became "a mode of thought in Western civilization," buttressed by eugenics, social Darwinism, and explicitly racist theories such as those of Count Gobineau. Primordialism serving the interests of whites made the domination of darker peoples seem inescapable.[4]

Black inferiority was projected as a rationale for subordination, as "the destiny of the blacks." Publication of Gobineau's racist

2. Sultanov, "Nuclear Nightmares and Colonial Crimes," para. 2, 4.
3. Marx, *Making Race and Nation*, 3.
4. Marx, *Making Race and Nation*, 3.

theory in 1956, supported interpretations of Darwin as suggesting that "blacks were a degenerate race with no future."[5]

A major reason for the mistreatment of African natives was the belief that humans have evolved from some ape-like pre-ancestor, and that some human groups are less evolved than other human groups. For most of history, the dominant belief, at least in the Christian-Muslim-Judean world, was that all humans were offspring of our first parents, Adam and Eve. Consequently, in the eyes of God, and therefore, in the understanding of the churches, mosques, and synagogues, all humans are equal. This worldview was rejected as a result of Darwinian influence and gave birth to Darwinism's "child," eugenics. In the words of Darwin's disciple Herbert Spencer, "Superior hereditary traits made the 'dominant races' better fit to survive than the 'inferior races.'"[6] Furthermore, "longing for ideas to justify the nation's growing inequities, American elites firmly embraced Charles Darwin and fell head over heels for Herbert Spencer."[7] This history has been summarized by Professor Hamel:

> Not until the Western European Enlightenment and the rise of empirical science did the religious account of the origins of race start to crumble, only to give rise, unfortunately, to racist, pseudoscientific concepts of human classifications based on the distortions of Darwin's theory, namely social Darwinism.[8]

This change was comparatively rapid. Early in the transformation process, the "eugenics program won the support of the medical community," not only in Nazi Germany but in much of Europe, including France. Eugenics "was part of a much broader racial purification process that was intended to exterminate human beings deemed to be deviant, degenerate, diseased, disordered, or otherwise 'devoid of value,'" especially including native

5. Marx, *Making Race and Nation*, 59.

6. Kendi, *Stamped from the Beginning*, 210.

7. Kendi, *Stamped from the Beginning*, 210.

8. Hamel, *Black Morocco*, 77.

Africans.[9] Darwin called the "Natives of southern Africa and their descendants 'the lowest savages.'"[10] For example, the Algerians were viewed as

> symbols of barbarity, threats and backwardness, while their disappearance would soon be reconstituted into equally broad sets of conceptual and structural goals in the writing of officers for whom killing was a question of revenge, strategy, or the playing out of Darwinian necessity. To take a more specific example, the massacre of tribes was often construed as a beneficent act in that the lives of smaller numbers of individuals were sacrificed for larger progressive goals, which France's unknown victims ought to understand would be shared by their kin as much as their killers'.[11]

The massacre was such that no more than a hundred French soldiers died in battle out of an army numbering tens of thousands, while the "number of Algerians perishing was in the order of tens of thousands."[12] Professor Gallois commented on "the manner in which ethnic extinctions were countenanced in the new science," that "wherever the European has trod, death seems to pursue the aboriginal. . . . The varieties of man seem to act on each other; in the same way as [with] different species of animals, the stronger always extirpating the weaker."[13]

French scientist Professor Olivier Le Cour Grandmaison stated, regarding Algeria,

> The massacre, extermination, the complete disappearance of others, is not a crime but the result of the struggle between the superior and inferior races, whose inferiority necessarily leads to a just form of annihilation.[14]

9 Chorover, *Genesis to Genocide*, 80.

10. Marx, *Making Race and Nation*, 3.

11. Gallois, *History of Violence*, 10.

12. Gallois, *History of Violence*, 14.

13. Gallois, *History of Violence*, 149.

14. Gallois, *History of Violence*, 149.

The French leadership observed,

> The first step towards colonization was the extermination of indigenous peoples. In the case of Algeria, if the complete extermination of the Algerian population was not possible, then at the very least the British example in America should be followed, with partial extermination and the complete dispersal (refoulement) of local populations.[15]

These "pure race" ideas "were seriously entertained in both medical and governmental circles for more than a quarter-century before the Nazis came to power."[16] The goals of "racial purification, for which social biological concepts provided a supposedly scientific justification and an explicit formulation indispensable for purposes of public indoctrination," would allow Europeans to support the genocide programs that were aggressively carried out by the European powers.[17]

The "superior race" ideology has existed for centuries, but it was not until Darwin that these ideas became "science" and were widely implemented by Western powers. Using modern weapons of war allowed the slaughter of millions who had little defense except spears, knives, and arrows, which were no match for the European's powerful muskets and cannons.[18] Lerner writes,

> For at least two thousand years of recorded history, social actions have been implemented based on the belief that certain people had something inherent in them, something in their blood, that made them less than human and consequently deserving of persecution or even death. It was not until the mid-nineteenth century, however, that this doctrine became broadly legitimated in society and science. Several intellectual events gave rise to this prominence. First and most important was Charles Darwin's view of evolution, involving the ideas

15. Gallois, *History of Violence*, 146.

16. Chorover, *Genesis to Genocide*, 80.

17. Chorover, *Genesis to Genocide*, 81.

18. Neba-Fuh, *Triumph of Racism*.

of natural selection, survival of the fittest, and continuity in the biological heritage of animal and human—that is, of the descent of humans from prehuman ancestors.[19]

Dr. Ethel Tobach, founder of *Psychologists for Social Action*, added that colonization and genocidal massacres often proceeded in tandem, adding that the

> concept of Social Darwinism had its explicit beginnings in the evolutionary thought of [Darwinist Herbert] Spencer. His phrase "survival of the fittest" referred to cultures, but was adopted by Darwin to explicate the process of natural selection. . . . The amalgamation of Spencer's concept with Darwin's theory of the evolution of species produced a seemingly scientific rationalization for the 19th century European and American view of the peoples of the world as two populations, one of which was superior to the other by reason of physical and mental characteristics. This rationalization came to be known as Social Darwinism. . . . Since the development of Social Darwinism, the concept of active human innervation in the evolutionary process of natural election has been adopted by many biologists, psychologists, and sociologists.[20]

THE ALGERIAN GENOCIDE

The application of the "survival of the fittest" worldview in Algeria illustrates the enormous harm caused by social Darwinism. The war between what Darwin called the superior and inferior races, i.e., the French and the Algerians, respectively, lasted for over a century. It only formally ended with Algeria's independence from France in 1962.[21] During the first three decades of French conquests in Algeria alone, the French army, totaling over five hundred thousand troops, killed between five hundred thousand and

19. Lerner, *Final Solutions*, 11.

20. Tobach et al., *Four Horsemen*, 99.

21. Gallois, *History of Violence*.

one million Algerians out of a total population of three million. The deaths were the result of massacres, war, starvation, and disease.[22] Atrocities committed by the French against Algerians included killing unarmed civilians, rape, torture, executions through "death flights," and being buried alive.[23]

Forced engagements by the French in wholesale massacres of entire tribes resulted in the extermination of eight tribes.[24] One well-documented example was the strict instructions given by the French general-in-chief Duc de Rovigo to the expeditionary body of troops, who were tasked with slaughtering the El Ouffia civilians, not sparing women, children, or the elderly.[25] General Marquis de Faudoas arrived with Colonel Schauenburg and their horsemen on the night of April 6, 1832, at the El Ouffia village, while the tribe members were asleep in their tents.[26] Most of General Faudoas's horsemen followed their orders not to make distinctions regarding the age or sex of their Algerian victims. Both swords and firearms were used to commit the mass murder of civilians. Reports document that boiling water was taken from cooking pots and tossed onto the Algerians by dismounted French cavalry.[27] All five hundred El Ouffian tribesmen, women, and children were slaughtered in a single night, and seven hundred members of the Ouled Rhia tribe were also killed soon after, mostly by suffocation. Only the actions of some sympathetic French soldiers, who disobeyed their orders, saved a few Algerian civilians. Another report related that the

> French army, by order of General Clauzel, issued an order to its military units to besiege the town of Blida under the pretext of boycotting its residents from selling food to the colonial authorities. They killed approximately 2,000

22. Neba-Fuh, *Triumph of Racism*.

23. McDougall, *History of Algeria*.

24. Kiernan, *Blood and Soil*, 305.

25. Nasrallah, "Documented Examples of French Crimes."

26. Grad, *L'Alsace*.

27. McDougall, *History of Algeria*.

Algerians, most of whom were women and children, and turned the city into a mass grave.[28]

In only a few hours, the entire city was reduced to a cemetery. Not a single survivor remained.

> French General Cavaignac then bragged that he had annihilated the entire Beni Sabih tribe. People were driven into a cave, then fires were lit at the entrance, causing most of those in the cave to suffocate. Those few who managed to escape were captured and murdered in the same manner.[29]

The Awlad Riyah tribe met a similar fate after rebelling against French cruelty under General Pelissier. More than a thousand civilians died from suffocation in the Farashish cave. Up to two million Algerian civilians were deported to internment camps, which concentrated large segments of the rural population, including entire villages and tribes, under military supervision to prevent them from aiding what the French called a "rebellion."[30] The

> French white supremacy policy of continuity is revealed in the number of French military interventions in Africa. . . . It has thousands of specialized soldiers active across the continent and has intervened over 40 times to bring down legitimate governments that threaten its interests.[31]

THE MADAGASCAR MASSACRE

Madagascar is an island off the southeast coast of Africa, located in the Indian Ocean. It is the world's fourth-largest island, and it was largely under the control of the Kingdom of Imerina. The king's royal palaces were located in the capital, a city named

28. Nasrallah, "Documented Examples of French Crimes," 78.

29. Nasrallah, "Documented Examples of French Crimes," 78.

30. Maran, *Torture*.

31. Neba-Fuh, *Triumph of Racism*, 536.

Antananarivo.[32] After several failed attempts to control the island, in September of 1894, France used military force to capture the royal palace. In February 1895, they exiled Prime Minister Rainilaiarivony and declared Madagascar a French colony.[33]

As was true of the other French colonies in Africa, the White rulers and Black natives produced the superior and inferior dichotomy.[34] The life experience of workers was shaped by racial ideologies, which, in turn, reshaped the society.[35] Typical was the comment by one author who opined that the Europeans, especially Frenchmen, had a "duty to civilize 'savage races' and to make sure that the whole globe was inhabited only by civilized men."[36] The racism established by the French many decades ago still has repercussions even today, including the belief that those who are more African in appearance are biologically inferior.[37]

The "Madagascar Massacre" refers to the French colonial repression and violence against the Malagasy population, particularly during the 1947–1948 revolt. In April 1947, eighteen thousand soldiers were stationed in Madagascar, which increased to thirty thousand in 1948 to suppress the revolt. The revolt was a response to the inhumanely harsh conditions imposed by French colonial rule, including forcing natives into slave labor on French-owned plantations. The revolt was fueled by racism, xenophobia, and colonialist ideals, resulting in torching entire villages, widespread killing, torture, and war rape by French soldiers. Some living Malagasy prisoners were tossed out of flying airplanes.[38]

Jacques Rabemananjara led an effort to achieve independence for Madagascar through legal channels. The failure of this initiative, and the harsh response it drew from the Ramadier administration, radicalized elements of the Malagasy population, including several

32. Neba-Fuh, *Triumph of Racism*, 243.
33. Neba-Fuh, *Triumph of Racism*, 243.
34. Saada, *Empire's Children*, 137, 180, 262, 306.
35. Savage, *From Slavery to Indenture*.
36. Cohen, *French Encounter with Africans*, 273.
37. Joy, "Western Influence, Latent Racism."
38. Neba-Fuh, *Triumph of Racism*, 245.

nationalist leaders. The rebels were poorly armed. Only a few natives had rifles, and most natives faced the modern French military with spears.[39]

The Democratic Movement for Malagasy Renewal (MDRM), the main indigenous political party, launched an independence movement in 1946 by assembling a three-hundred-thousand-member resistance force. The MDRM was soon dissolved, and its members were tried before French military courts; many were given death sentences. In the end, around forty thousand died or were murdered. The people who had taken refuge in the forests came out of their hiding places in a state of misery.[40]

A BRIEF NOTE ON CAMEROON AND MOROCCO

The same inhumane treatment could be mentioned for the other French colonies, but only two will be mentioned. Although the French did not aim for the systematic destruction of the Moroccans, unlike what occurred during the French conquest of Algeria, French forces killed up to one hundred thousand people to suppress revolts in Morocco.[41] Cameroon, formerly a German colony, is a Central African country most famously known for its diverse natural landscapes and cultural richness. It is 475,000 square kilometers (184,000 square miles) in size—about the size of California. In Cameroon, the Union des populations du Cameroun (UPC), a pro-independence party supported by the people, faced the wrath of the French administration, resulting in the 1948–1971 Bamilekes genocide, when French soldiers exterminated four hundred thousand Cameroonians. The Bamileke people were a Central African ethnic group ruled by about one hundred chiefdoms in the Western Province of Cameroon.[42]

39. Howard, "Revolt in Madagascar."
40. Howard, "Revolt in Madagascar."
41. Hamel, *Black Morocco*, 235.
42. Hamel, *Black Morocco*, 235.

According to Max Bardet, who served from 1962–1964 as a pilot in Cameroon, the army targeted the Bamileke people who supported the UPC. It was a ruthless war involving bombing villages and killing women and children. The French then carried out "systematic torture" of the Bamilekes. The officers involved wanted to be reassured that there were no witnesses to the slaughter so as not to implicate France. Buttressed by "the ideology of social Darwinism," the French bombed villages and rounded up hundreds of thousands of villagers, who were forced to assemble in areas behind barbed wire, then were slaughtered like animals.[43]

Not even the English-speaking area escaped the French assault, who blamed the British for hiding nationalists. Using this excuse as justification, they illegally penetrated British Cameroon to carry out targeted assassinations while blaming London for fomenting unrest in French colonies. The same story was repeated for most of the French colonies.[44]

Italy colonized portions of Libya, Eritrea, and Somalia, and, in 1936, briefly occupied Ethiopia, forming Italian East Africa (in the Horn of Africa).

Spain colonized primarily two main territories in Africa: Equatorial Guinea and parts of Morocco. While other areas, like Western Sahara (a disputed territory on the northwest coast of Africa) and Ifni (on the Atlantic coast of Morocco, south of Agadir and across from the Canary Islands), were also under Spanish control at different times, these were not independent countries.[45]

SUMMARY

This chapter can only briefly summarize the central importance of Darwinism and the rejection of Genesis in inspiring and justifying the brutal treatment and exploitation of millions of native Africans. A more complete work by Neba-Fuh, encompassing 678

43. Neba-Fuh, *Triumph of Racism*, 280, 285.
44. Hamel, *Black Morocco*, 235.
45. Hamel, *Black Morocco*, 235.

6.5″ × 11″ small-print pages, in great detail, documents the results of European control of all of the countries in Africa. His summary, based on a much larger sample than I used, is the same as mine. He concluded that "racism played a major role in Europe's" abuse of the African people.[46] Specifically,

> Europe's demonization of Africans as inferior, worthless, uncivilized, primitive beings that were not different than animals, led to the exhibition of caged Africans in Western zoos. These racist, demonizing tendencies ultimately became the justification for the barbaric and dehumanizing Trans-Atlantic slave trade. Following huge profits derived from the blood and sweat of enslaved Africans, white supremacy leaders came together at the Berlin conference.[47]

"Lieutenant General Lothar von Trotha, the Commander-in-Chief of the Schutztruppe in German South West Africa, with his staff in Keetmanshoop during the Herero Uprising."[48]

46. Neba-Fuh, *Triumph of Racism*, 535.

47. Neba-Fuh, *Triumph of Racism*, 535.

48. Bundesarchiv, Bild 183-R27576, Unknown author, CC-BY-SA 3.0, from Wikimedia Commons: https://commons.wikimedia.org/wiki/File:Bundesarchiv_Bild_183-R27576,_Deutsch-S%C3%BCdwestafrika,_Herero-Aufstand.jpg.

8

Darwinism's South African Holocaust

DARWINISM-INSPIRED RACISM HAS HAD an adverse influence on every nation in Africa, including South Africa.[1] Specifically, Darwin's writings were used as a powerful support for the genocide of the native African peoples.[2] Darwin wrote, "At some future period, not very distant, the civilized races of man will almost certainly exterminate and replace the savage races."[3] As Fredrickson documented, "The Darwinist concept of racial degeneracy and extinction provided the 'scientific' basis for most of the virulent anti-Negro propaganda that spewed forth in unprecedented volume around the turn of the century."[4] Anthropologist David Graeber and archaeologist David Wengrow, as professors, observed the fact that "the publication of Darwin's theories meant that evolutionism became entrenched as the only possible scientific approach to history—or at least the only one likely to be given credence in universities."[5]

1. Dubow, *Science and Society*.
2. Barta, "Mr. Darwin's Shooters."
3. Darwin, *Descent of Man*, 201.
4. Fredrickson, *Black Image*, 256.
5. Graeber and Wengrow, *Dawn of Everything*, 446.

The formally defined reason for genocide is to serve utilitarian purposes, namely extinction "as a means to gain access to land and other resources."[6] This definition perfectly describes the genocide of African Blacks. Tulane professor William Benjamin Smith noted, "The details of anatomical argument, which Darwin said would undoubtedly lead the naturalist to classify Negro and European as distinct species, are matters of readily accessible knowledge."[7]

To treat native Africans as an inferior race, justifying genocide, the "white man has to see him as a beast, a black animal."[8] The racism that produced genocide, the kind of racism of White against Black Africans, asserts that Black Africans "are not merely an inferior race, but a different animal altogether."[9] In support of this idea, Langbehn and Salama wrote that "racism denies that humans belong to a common species. There are different races in the same way [that] there are different kinds of animals."[10] And displaying these animals in zoos, as frequently happened, allows Westerners to view these "animals" in their natural setting.[11] The end result of this perception, both in Nazi Germany and as a result of colonialism in Africa, was genocide.[12] Fortunately, the Christian influence among the ruling White population has prevented the occurrence of another Nazi scale holocaust in South Africa.[13] Nonetheless, "scientific racism, eugenics, and Social Darwinism . . . [all] played important roles in justifying white supremacy."[14]

Scientific Darwinism in South Africa allowed many Whites to rationalize their racist policies. Furthermore, according to John Whitson Cell, professor of history at Duke University, "Servitude

6. Sarkin, *Colonial Genocide and Reparations Claims*, 104.

7. Smith, *Color Line*, 45.

8. Kiernan, *Blood and Soil*, 36, 375.

9. Langbehn and Salama, *German Colonialism*, 103.

10. Langbehn and Salama, *German Colonialism*, 103.

11. Blanchard et al., *Human Zoos*.

12. Langbehn and Salama, *German Colonialism*, 103.

13. Rich, "Race, Science, and the Legitimization," 667.

14. Dubow, *Science and Society*, 2.

and the Darwinian struggle for existence both became more acceptable to conscience when the victims could be identified as subhuman."[15] The sad fact is Social Darwinism and conclusions regarding race "fitness" were widely accepted in South Africa by both English- and Afrikaans-speaking race ideologues.[16] Mainstream biological scientific racism, widely supported by scientific experts both in the United States and South Africa, impelled racial segregationist movements in South Africa.[17]

Behind their thinking "was the assumption that there was some form of order and hierarchy in human races in which the white, Anglo-Saxon race occupied the topmost position."[18] Although some of the "Social Darwinists in South Africa held that Africans would completely die out in the face of advancing white colonial settlement," most realized that the White population was, and would remain for decades, a distinct numerical minority.[19]

The two most influential thinkers of the nineteenth century, Karl Marx and Charles Darwin, focused on class struggle.[20] Darwin taught that, in the struggle for existence between the races, the "strongest must win in the end. . . . Such observations were particularly widespread in relation to the conquest of Africa."[21] Charles Darwin

> famously included a chapter on "The Extinction of the Races of Man" in *The Descent of Man* (1871) and many writers in the mid-nineteenth century justified the "disappearance" of "primitive races" on evolutionary grounds.[22]

15. Cell, *Highest Stage of White Supremacy*, 4.

16. Rich, "Race, Science, and the Legitimization," 665.

17. Rich, "Race, Science, and the Legitimization," 669.

18. Rich, "Race, Science, and the Legitimization," 667.

19. Rich, "Race, Science, and the Legitimization," 667.

20. Claeys, *Cambridge Companion to Nineteenth-Century*.

21. Claeys, *Cambridge Companion to Nineteenth-Century*, 163, 172.

22. Moses, *Empire, Colony, Genocide*, 164.

The result of the belief in Darwin's "Favoured Races" was that the African natives, deemed by European Whites as a less evolved race compared to the Whites, were unfit to govern the land they hold and therefore must eventually give way before the irresistible advance of the stronger White people.[23] The result was that, during the nineteenth century, an estimated 4.2 million native Africans were either massacred or died from diseases, including smallpox, measles, influenza, and typhus, brought by the Europeans during colonization.[24]

Although social Darwinists believed that native Africans would become extinct in the face of advancing White colonial settlements, it was also held that this was *not due to the White colonial settlements*, but rather, as "Darwin argued . . . species become extinct because they fail to adapt" to environmental changes.[25] Western society has regarded itself as the "civilized races," while the native inhabitants of the colonies were regarded as the "savage races."[26] This idea became the foundation of the South African white supremacy movement.

Armed with the eminent "scientific" Darwinian authority, many Western countries and individuals began to oppress and otherwise discriminate against the "inferior" native populations. It was widely accepted that Darwin had clear scientific support for his "famous conclusion . . . that the gulf between savages and civilized humans is almost unbridgeable."[27] Thus, many Whites were influenced to view the gap as unbridgeable, a view that supported their material self-interest.

Professor Duerden's approach to the White-Black race "problem" was as follows: "History shows that, when in any numbers a superior race comes into contact with an inferior race, one of

23. Claeys, *Cambridge Companion to Nineteenth-Century*, 172.

24. Olusoga and Erichsen, *Kaiser's Holocaust*; Hochschild, *King Leopold's Ghost*.

25. Langbehn and Salama, *German Colonialism*, 101.

26. Oluniyi, *Darwin Comes to Africa*.

27. Brantlinger, *Dark Vanishings*, 165.

three things may happen."[28] The *superior* race will usually (1) exterminate or (2) force into slavery the *inferior* race, or (3) the two races will adapt to each other and learn to live together. He was not optimistic about the third possibility occurring. Duerden concluded that it will be a triumph for white civilization if they can raise primitive people up to the level of the whites.[29] His use of terms such as "inferior" and "superior" did not help to facilitate the two groups living in peace.

South African racism was unique because most cases of Darwinism-inspired discrimination have been against the minority race, as was the case in Nazi Germany. However, in contrast to Nazi Germany, the race believed to be inferior in South Africa was the numerically dominant race, Black Africans. "The history of scientific racism in South Africa has been overlooked" partly because the embarrassing history was "deliberately downplayed,"[30] since the apartheid goal was to separate the social, educational, and developmental lines between the Black and White populations. The major limitation to implementing this goal was that Black labor was required to run the economy.

Scientific racism, eugenics, and social Darwinism all played critical roles in justifying white supremacy, which produced an epidemic of murder. As Darwin's ideas were becoming more widely accepted, they "began to challenge the orthodox truths of Christian scripture" and, concurrently, "Darwinian ideas were reshaping theories of evolution" and "the science of race, which slip-streamed in Darwin's wake, was given particular impetus by the imperial conquest in South Africa."[31]

Importantly, "for Darwin, natural selection was a purely mechanical phenomenon that, devoid of all purpose, was marked by pitiless indifference to the human condition."[32] Natural selection produced a "pitiless struggle in the animal world," which many

28. Duerden, "Genetics and Eugenics," 68.

29. Duerden, "Genetics and Eugenics," 76.

30. Dubow, *Scientific Racism*, 4.

31. Beinart and Dubow, *Scientific Imagination in South Africa*, 10–11.

32. Dubow, *Science and Society*, 27.

evolutionists applied to Blacks, whom, as noted above, were regarded by many Darwinists as animals.[33] Furthermore, Darwinism fostered anti-Christian philosophies, such as secularism and scientism, that undermine the Adam and Eve biblical teaching.[34]

DARWINISM SUPPORTED BY LEADING ACADEMICS

During the last century, in much of the world, Darwinian ideas were supported by many leading academics. This included many Afrikaan academics like P. J. Coertze, professor of Volkekunde (ethnology) at the University of Pretoria, South Africa, and Raymond Dart, the discoverer of Java Man, widely touted by some as the "missing link," a claim which was later disproved.[35]

Darwinian ideas also began to permeate South African education. In 1935, University of Witwatersrand geneticist Gerrie Eloff, drawing heavily on German eugenist Eugen Fischer's anthropological studies, advocated eugenic "breeding" to produce a more fit race. Citing the work of zoologist H. B. Fantham, a "passionate eugenist," Fischer also condemned interbreeding with inferior races because they produced "black-white racial mixtures and [he believed] . . . that 'hybrids' were mentally, physically, and morally inferior to their white progenitors."[36] As Rich stressed,

> The scientific popularisers of race looked for tendencies described by Philip Curtin as "diversificationism," which emphasized aspects of human difference rather than similarity. Behind much of their thinking was the assumption that there was some form of order and hierarchy in human races in which the white, Anglo-Saxon race occupied the topmost position.[37]

---

33. Dubow, *Science and Society*, 26.

34. Dubow, *Science and Society*, 14.

35. Dubow, *Scientific Racism*, 103.

36. Dubow, *Scientific Racism*, 272.

37. Rich, "Race, Science, and the Legitimization," 667.

One example was the former vice president of the Royal Anthropological Institute, British anthropologist A. H. Keane. Keane was "a virulent racist who dismissed Africans as [being] of low intellectual capacity."[38] In 1909, Keane declared that African natives had "ceased to evolve" compared to Whites in the past, and therefore were now "incapable of development."[39]

As evidence, Keane cited Virginia physician Robert W. Shufeldt's work *The Negro: A Menace to American Civilization*. The book was very popular among both American and South African segregationists. Leading Darwinist Frederick W. Bell referred to Shufeldt as "the greatest authority in America on the mental capacity and social status of the Negro," arguing that "the South African native belongs to a distinctly lower race than the White man."[40]

Shufeldt used fossil comparisons to conclude that

> [the average Negro is] intellectually about midway between the human precursor (early Pliocene man) and the present most-advanced civilized people; in other words, he lags, in terms of time, at least one million years behind [the average White man].[41]

In his books, Shufeldt often credited the works of Darwin and other leading evolutionists for his conclusions.[42]

THE 1899–1902 BRITISH-BOER WAR

Race was central in the South African War between the British and Boer republics. Although outnumbered, the Boers (meaning "farmers") were a tenacious and determined enemy.[43] After a long period of guerrilla warfare, the ten thousand British troops

38. Rich, "Race, Science, and the Legitimization," 671.

39. Quoted in Rich, "Race, Science, and the Legitimization," 672.

40. Quoted in Dubow, *Scientific Racism*, 92.

41. Shufeldt, *America's Greatest Problem*, 51.

42. Shufeldt, *America's Greatest Problem*, 10, 13, 26, 29, 30, 34, 36, 42, 80, 84, 85.

43. Scholtz, *Why the Boers Lost*.

eventually prevailed by pursuing a "scorched earth," "survival-of-the-fittest" strategy that involved burning Boer farms and forcing their wives and children into concentration camps, where about thirty thousand died from disease and malnutrition.[44] Furthermore, Professor Cell wrote,

> The late nineteenth century was the age of Social Darwinism, when professors of history in Germany and elsewhere described the grand struggle of nations in the past and looked forward to its speedy and glorious renewal. War was clean, manly, and vigorous, a purifying fire.[45]

The 1909 Act of Union, which was designed to settle the conflict, actually made the situation far worse because it gave the White government extensive control over the Black population.[46] Furthermore, about 90 percent of the land was given to the million Whites and a mere 7.3 percent was restricted to the four million South African Blacks.[47]

As was true of most African colonies ruled by Whites, the South Africa conflict was framed in the language of Darwinian "scientific" racism.[48] Typical is the claim that science has discovered the

> remarkable innate physiological intellectual capacities [and] differences between the brain of the White man of European descent and that of the Bantu—differences which are innate and constitute the measure of their respective intellectual capacities. . . . Today science brings us proofs that the cerebral capacities of what we call the "native" are, when he has reached the age of puberty, distinctly inferior in comparison with those of the white children.[49]

---

44. Hasian, "'Hysterical' Emily Hobhouse."

45. Cell, *Highest Stage of White Supremacy*, 4.

46. Arnold, *Africa*, 331.

47. Arnold, *Africa*, 330.

48. Arnold, *Africa*, 74.

49. Quoted in Dubow, *Scientific Racism*, 269.

Two systems of concentration camps existed during the British-Boer War, one for Blacks and another one for Whites. Because Victorian sentiment at the time was racially guided, the conditions in the two camps were very different. The main difference was the politically driven race politics. Most of the concentration camp deaths were a result of disease that took the most vulnerable, mainly children.[50] Furthermore,

> water supplies were often contaminated by disease, and proper medical attention was rare to non-existent. Abhorrent sub-human conditions meant that water-borne diseases like dysentery, typhoid and diarrhea spread with ease and the death rate climbed drastically.[51]

Furthermore, the administration of the camps provided food of poor quality and tolerated generally unhygienic conditions. Consequently, African civilians suffered terribly.

Eventually, twenty-eight thousand Boer women and children and, in addition, at least twenty thousand Blacks died due the poor conditions in the camps.[52] The brutal experiences of the Blacks were simply brushed aside with a large degree of apathy. Even after the Boer War, poor treatment of Blacks persisted, including during apartheid.

THE PROBLEM OF BRITISH RACISM

This is only one of many examples of British racism based on the inferior race belief inspired by Darwin. After all, Darwin was British. Britain's twentieth century empire was the largest in human history. It included a quarter of the world's land and nearly seven hundred million people.[53] As true of the French and Germans, the British relied on the Darwinian racial hierarchy to justify their brutality.

50. Dickins, "'BLACK' Concentration Camps."
51. Dickins, "'BLACK' Concentration Camps," para. 37.
52. Pretorius, "Boer Wars."
53. Elkins, *Legacy of Violence.*

The best African example of Britain's mistreatment of the native people was the British Gulag in Kenya. Kenya was "organized according to a strongly hierarchical scale of humanity. The majority of Africans were at the very bottom of the European settlers' human hierarchy."[54] In short,

> skin color became the mark of difference. Whites were at one end of civilization's spectrum, Blacks at the other. All other shades of humanity fell somewhere between, and skin pigment was the visible brand of cultural difference.[55]

The British firmly believed in their own

> racial superiority that infused every rung of the colony's white socioeconomic ladder. By virtue of their skin color, whites of all classes were the master race and therefore deserving of privilege. To the settlers there was nothing noble about the African "savage." Many believed the African to be biologically inferior, with smaller brain sizes, [and] a limited capacity to feel pain or emotion.[56]

White racial superiority in Kenya had long manifested itself in various kinds of primitive settler justice, including public floggings, beating deaths, and summary executions. The result of this inferior belief was described by Harvard University historian Caroline Elkins. She described in detail the "horrific crimes that occurred in defense of British rule in Kenya," including giving the victims electric shocks using car batteries as the source. Furthermore,

> they tied suspects to vehicle bumpers with just enough rope to drag them to death. They employed burning [victims with] cigarettes, fire, and hot coals. They thrust bottles (often broken), gun barrels, knives, snakes, vermin, sticks, and hot eggs up men's rectums and into women's vaginas. They crushed bones and teeth: sliced

54. Elkins, *Imperial Reckoning*, 47.
55. Elkins, *Imperial Reckoning*, 12.
56. Elkins, *Imperial Reckoning*, 12.

off fingers or their tips; and castrated men with specially designed instruments or by beating a suspect's testicles "till the scrotum burst," according to Anglican church offices. Some used a *kiboko*, or a rhino whip, for beating; others used clubs, fists, and truncheons.[57]

In fact, "social Darwinism" created a "unique view of the world that was embedded at every level of popular culture" even in methods used to deal with "inferior races."[58] Social Darwinism clearly had a major role in how the Whites treated the "inferior" race."[59]

ACADEMIC SUPPORT FOR RACISM

Following the "publication of Charles Darwin's book *On the Origin of Species by Natural Selection: Or the Preservation of Favoured Races in the Struggle for Life*, a view of races as evolving subspecies began to emerge."[60] The next step in the development of scientific racism was support from leading academics who concluded that "racism was constituted as a genetic trait and racial separation was the key to in-group success."[61] Darwin gave "the new racism the appearance of science," which, as we recognize today, was not science but social Darwinism.[62] Academics were "firmly of the view that Black people were intellectually inferior to whites."[63] This Darwinian belief motivated many in academia to support both racism and apartheid.[64] Furthermore, once the label of science was applied, a large number of South African academics supported the racist movement that led to the exploitation of Blacks. Although a

57. Elkins, *Legacy of Violence*, 556.

58. Elkins, *Legacy of Violence*, 352.

59. Stocking, *Race, Culture, and Evolution*.

60. Manzo, *Creating Boundaries*, 59.

61. Manzo, *Creating Boundaries*, 58.

62. Barker, *The New Racism*, 78.

63. Beinart and Dubow, *Scientific Imagination in South Africa*, 100.

64. Turner, "Eugenic Underpinnings."

few creationists existed, even in academia, "Darwinian ideas were nevertheless gaining currency," especially after Darwin's *Descent of Man* book was published in 1871.[65]

One of the contradictions within academia was the belief that social deviance and/or low IQ scores in the poor White community were due to social conditions. Substantial resources were committed to correcting these conditions to ameliorate the problem. In contrast, the same conditions in the Black community were believed to be the result of biological and heredity.[66]

The belief that "mental deficiency was primarily caused by heredity" (as were harmful vices and pauperism) was widely held by leading academics.[67] The head of the University of Pretoria sociology department, Dr. Geoffrey Cronjé (1907–1922), wrote several books supporting the view that, in the end, eugenics was the only solution to crime and most other social evils. He was also the author of a "series of influential, widely read books" advocating the belief that marriage between the White and Black races produces physically and mentally inferior progeny.[68] Dutch-born physiologist A. J. Janse went further and concluded that *only* by regulating marriage along eugenic lines would South Africa be prevented from becoming a country dominated by inferior races.[69]

Furthermore, he taught that "the mixing of blood between White and Black races *produces inferior human material in biological terms.*"[70] Cronjé's goal was to protect the "purity" of the nation's blood. He was strongly influenced by Gerrie Eloff, a South African zoologist and geneticist at the University of Witwatersrand in Johannesburg in the 1930s. Eloff was then the most prominent race scientist and eugenist in South Africa. His eminence was such that his ideas were given semi-official status in the influential

65. Beinart and Dubow, *Scientific Imagination in South Africa*, 104.

66. Duerden, "Genetics and Eugenics," 76.

67. Dubow, *Scientific Racism*, 148.

68. Dubow, *Scientific Racism*, 274.

69. Dubow, *Scientific Racism*, 173. Quoting Janse, "White and Black."

70. Dubow, *Scientific Racism in Modern South Africa*, 275. Emphasis in original.

nationalist movement. Eloff also condemned interbreeding and drew heavily on the anthropological studies by one of the leading Nazi eugenists Eugen Fischer.

Another Pretoria professor, W. A. Willemse, concluded that White and Black marriages produced both physically and mentally inferior humans, writing, "Miscegenation between whites and non-whites is . . . shown by biological research to be detrimental."[71] In contrast to this claim, miscegenation between Whites and non-Whites has now been empirically shown by biological research to be, in general, beneficial for the offspring.[72]

One of the earlier advocates of the "full gospel of eugenics" was the zoology and comparative anatomy professor at the University of Witwatersrand, Harold B. Fantham. As early as 1918, he was promoting in South Africa the evolutionary principles administered by eugenic "experts." He believed that human advancement depended on the conservation of the "good human germ plasm" and the eradication of "defective genes."[73] Based on Darwin's ideas, he argued against providing humanitarian and social services to Black Africans, believing that these interventions would lead to racial degeneration. He was inspired by the following words of Charles Darwin:

> With savages, the weak in body or mind are soon eliminated; and those that survive commonly exhibit a vigorous state of health. We civilized men, on the other hand, do our utmost to check the process of elimination; we build asylums for the imbecile, the maimed, and the sick; we institute poor-laws; and our medical men exert their utmost skill to save the life of every one to the last moment. . . . Vaccination has preserved thousands, who from a weak constitution would formerly have succumbed to smallpox. Thus, the weak members of civilized societies propagate their kind. No one who has attended to the breeding of domestic animals will doubt that this must be highly injurious to the race of man. It is surprising

71. Cronjé, 'n Tuiste vir die Nageslag, 74.

72. Latson, "Biracial Advantage"; Johnson, "Darwin's Legacy."

73. Rich, "Race, Science, and the Legitimization," 677.

> how soon a want of care, or care wrongly directed, leads
> to the degeneration of a domestic race; but excepting in
> the case of man himself, hardly anyone is so ignorant as
> to allow his worst animals to breed.[74]

Fantham brought considerable prestige to the eugenic movement by using Darwin to justify racism because he (Fantham) had

> graduated from Cambridge (Christ's College) and
> University College, London, where he had been a gold
> medallist in zoology and a Derby research scholar. A
> passionate eugenicist, Fantham established a school of
> research at Wits and served on the university's senate,
> as well as being dean of the science faculty. In a number
> of public lectures, he urged the need for sociologists to
> become "thoroughly versed in biological science" and
> outlined the basic precepts of eugenics and race fit-
> ness in terms of a Darwinian pattern of evolutionary
> development.[75]

IMPLEMENTATION OF SOCIAL DARWINISM

The implementation of social Darwinism in South African cities occurred as early as the 1870s. As a result, "the fear of plague and the language of biological contamination was an important part of the rationale for introducing urban segregation" of the races.[76] These segregation laws culminated in the Group Areas Act, which assigned separate living areas for Blacks and Whites. The result was ruthless uprooting of both mixed and homogenous communities by forced resettlement based on race.[77] The South African medical association's ruling that tuberculosis was hereditary was readily accepted by many Whites as justification to isolate the races.[78]

---

74. Darwin, *Descent of Man*, 168.

75. Rich, "Race, Science, and the Legitimization," 677.

76. Dubow, *Scientific Racism*, 129.

77. Johnson, "Darwin's legacy," 405.

78. Andersson, "Tuberculosis and Social Stratification."

Afrikaans literary giant, medical doctor C. Louis Leipoldt, edited the eugenic magazine *Social Hygiene* when he was a medical student. Although ambivalent about the biological determinism belief, he stated while he was the medical inspector of the Transvaal schools that the "most pressing question that clamours for an authoritative answer in Africa, South as well as Central, is whether the white race can maintain itself in the continent as the superior race."[79] The South African government established and financed *The Council for Scientific and Industrial Research*, whose mandate was to establish a "scientific" basis for racial differences.[80]

Native Affairs Society member Frederick W. Bell quoted British anthropologist A. H. Kean, who referred to Africans as the "lowest position in the evolutionary scale."[81] In 1908, he relied on British and American anthropologists to support the belief that Black Africans represented "the lowest position on the evolutionary scale" and that

> no full blooded negro has ever been distinguished as a man of science, a poet, or an artist, and the fundamental equality claimed for him by ignorant philanthropists is belied by the whole history of the race throughout the historical period.[82]

Bell both received support for his ideas from anthropologists Robert Broom, and wholehearted endorsement by the leading newspapers. He added that the smattering of European education that the Black Africans received "did not make them a civilized people because their education was nothing but a veneer."[83] In his trip to South Africa, "Sir George Darwin (the eugenicist son of Charles) . . . observed with satisfaction the dominance of the European race in . . . South Africa."[84] In the "field of eugenics and

79. Dubow, *Scientific Racism*, 174.

80. Dubow, *Scientific Racism*, 218.

81. Dubow, *Scientific Racism*, 90.

82. Dubow, *Scientific Racism*, 90.

83. Dubow, *Scientific Racism*, 90.

84. Beinart and Dubow, *Scientific Imagination in South Africa*, 161.

mental testing, practitioners of race psychology ... concluded that black People could not benefit from education on the same basis as whites."[85]

BUSHMEN: AN EVOLUTIONARY THROWBACK

Cambridge anthropologist A. C. Haddon openly wanted to research the primitive South Africans before they died off. In his presidential address to the anthropology section, he stressed that the "doomed 'primitive' people" in South Africa "merited thorough investigation before they disappeared."[86] The famous South African writer/educator Sir Laurens van der Post believed that the Bushmen were an evolutionary throwback whose bodies needed to be preserved as museum specimens to document evolutionary progress. Saul Dubow observed that, more than any other discipline, the physical anthropology discipline generated and sustained the racial paradigm in South Africa. The effect was to create the now-refuted ladder model of human evolution.[87]

> In the 1970s, human evolution was conceived of as being ladder-like: with one or two exceptions, fossil hominin species were considered to be rungs on a ladder that connected a common ancestor to modern humans. The species at the bottom of the ladder were more apelike, whereas the ones near the top were more like modern humans. We now know human evolution history is ... nonlinear; a better analogy is a bush. Only one stem of that bush has managed to survive to the present, and that is us, modern humans.[88]

85. Beinart and Dubow, *Scientific Imagination in South Africa*, 212.

86. Beinart and Dubow, *Scientific Imagination in South Africa*, 161.

87. Wood, "Paleo-Anthropology's Superstar," 327.

88. Wood, "Paleo-Anthropology's Superstar," 327.

LEADERS OF SOUTH AFRICA—DARWINISTS

Many of the leaders of South Africa were openly Darwinists. Typical is African Cecil John Rhodes (famous for the Rhodes scholarship), who wrote that the African Blacks were "'the laziest race under the sun' with few wants except the minimal hut tax."[89] He added, "It was really ridiculous to suppose that these poor children could be taken out of this absolute barbarism and . . . come to a practical conclusion on . . . politics."[90] The reason for their inferiority, Rhodes opined, was simple: "Their brains were different" from the Whites."[91] Rhodes naively accepted the so-called "race science" based on social Darwinism. One result of this evolutionary belief, apartheid (literally, "apart-hood," i.e., separateness), was

> the most elaborate racial edifice the world has ever seen. The basic structure of Apartheid rested on a Population Registration Act requiring every person to be assigned to one of three racial groups: White, Coloured, or African.[92]

Rhodes admitted that his exposure to Darwin was one basis of his racist ideas. Rhodes claimed that a book titled *The Martyrdom of Man*, by social Darwinist William Winwood Reade, was the bible for secularists.[93] William Reade journeyed to Africa to prove Darwin's theory, concluding that his study of the "savages" there confirmed Darwin.[94]

Reade, a self-labeled Darwin disciple, relied heavily on Herbert Spencer, T. H. Huxley, John Tyndall, John William Draper, and other leading evolutionists in his writings about evolution.[95]

Rhodes wrote that the English "are the finest race in the world and that the more of the world we [the English] inhabit, the better

89. Rotberg, *Founder*, 48.
90. Rotberg, *Founder*, 470.
91. Rotberg, *Founder*, 470.
92. Meredith, *Fortunes of Africa*, 582.
93. Rotberg, *Founder*, 100.
94. Reade, *Martyrdom of Man*, 4–5.
95. Reade, *Martyrdom of Man*, 5.

it is for the human race." He added that the Anglo-Saxon influence could vastly improve those parts of the world that are "at present inhabited by the most despicable specimens of human beings [the African Blacks]." He also opined that "Africa is still lying ready for us, [and] it is our duty to take it."[96]

Gresham's law as a monetary principle states that "bad money drives out good." Applying the law to people, it states that "inferior people drive out superior people." In contrast, eugenics theory has stressed that "the good was meant to drive out the bad, . . . construed in terms of a reverse of Gresham's law of Social Darwinism."[97] Apartheid was propelled by Darwinian, race-supremacist, eugenic ideas, and in

> an era of Social Darwinism and paternal imperialism, Rhodes' sweeping, chauvinistic program of expansion inspired a broad range of intimates and acquaintances to believe that the acquisition of chattels, goods, and territories could serve lofty, broad, and redeeming purpose.[98]

JAN CHRISTIAAN SMUTS

Former prime minister of the Union of South Africa Jan Christiaan Smuts (1870–1950) was a "subtle and relentless white supremacist."[99] Smut's support for Darwin was obvious. Darwin's books were prominently displayed alongside the books by evolutionist A. R. Wallace in his personal library at the Smuts Museum. In his 1929 lecture at Oxford University, Smuts opined that Africa was a human laboratory where the race science of anthropology could be practiced by studying the primitive people who lived there for many thousands of years without altering their body or mind.

Smuts opined that

96. Rotberg, *Founder*, 100.

97. Rotberg, *Founder*, 9, 530, 620.

98. Rotberg, *Founder*, 235–36.

99. Luthuli, *Let My People Go*, 101. See also Borstelmann, *Apartheid's Reluctant Uncle*, 35.

the first that it is we see, in the one, the leading race of the world, while the other, though still living, has become a mere human fossil, verging to extinction. We see the one crowned with all intellectual and spiritual glory of the race, while the other still occupies the lowest scale in human existence. If race has not played the difference, what has?[100]

Smuts even asserted that "there are certain things about which all South Africans agreed, all parties and all sections, except those who are quite mad. The first is, it is a fixed policy to maintain white supremacy in South Africa."[101] Smuts not even "once exerted his undoubted influence to extend a helping hand to the masses who groaned under their disabilities, and it was he who gave Hertzog the power to disenfranchise the few African voters."[102] Europeans had progressed, but in contrast, "the Bushman had remained isolated and static; but this was the luck of the evolutionary game."[103]

Daniël François Malan (1874–1959), the fourth prime minister of South Africa from 1948 until 1954, accepted social Darwinism.[104] He appealed to Herbert Spencer and other Social Darwinists as authorities for his governmental policy.[105] Malan opined that "whites and non-whites are not of the same kind."[106] Malan's successor, Johannes Gerhardus Strijdom (1893–1958), also accepted Darwinian racism, writing that "either the white man dominates, or the black man takes over. . . . The only way the European can maintain supremacy is by domination."[107]

The sixth prime minister of South Africa was Hendrik Verwoerd, who believed that differences in the "civilizational" progress of different races were described by theories of racial hierarchy

---

100. Smuts quoted in Dubow, *Scientific Racism*, 51.

101. Arnold, *Africa*, 330–31.

102. Luthuli, *Let My People Go*, 106.

103. Smuts quoted in Dubow, *Scientific Racism*, 51.

104. Koorts, *DF Malan*, 6.

105. Koorts, *DF Malan*, 7.

106. Koorts, *DF Malan*, 369.

107. Arnold, *Africa*, 331.

resulting from Darwinian ideas. Verwoerd's major policies had eugenic underpinnings. He advocated for separate education systems and other policies aimed at maintaining racial purity and preventing the mixing of races. In short, from the beginning of the twentieth century, social Darwinist theories were accepted by South African policy makers and politicians until fairly recently.[108]

SUMMARY

As elsewhere in the world, so in South Africa, Darwinism led to eugenics. It played a major role in determining winners and losers in business, education, sports, and politics through policy and legislation based on skin color. Racism in South Africa, supported by Darwinism, was also exploited to support social Darwinism.[109] The "survival of the fittest" doctrine was used to legitimize the right of Whites to settle on the continent of Africa and exploit its native people for over a century. For a "white public seeking to rationalize its social supremacy . . . a body of knowledge justifying racism was sufficient" to practice racism.[110]

Thus, pre-World War II Darwinian race-science claims fed into the racist white supremacist views of South African politics until very recently. They provided scientific authority for racist policies and legislation discreetly supported by the scientists and encouraged by the politicians. Evolutionary speculations led to the classification of people groups, which placed some groups in the "superior" category and others toward the "savage" end of the evolutionary scale.[111] Many scientists, intoxicated by the success of science, were happy to go along with the racism it supported. In the end, even extermination orders were at times issued by the

---

108. Beinart and Dubow, *Scientific Imagination in South Africa*, 177.
109. Manzo, *Creating Boundaries*, 57.
110. Dubow, *Scientific Racism*, 9.
111. Dubow, *Scientific Racism*, 85.

White rulers of African colonies. These orders led to over a million deaths, often by inhumane, brutal means.[112]

Actually, many Western world governments were anxious to place a scientific imprimatur on their racist policies from about 1880 to after World War II. However, after World War II, the racist worldview rapidly declined when the horrendous fruits of eugenics, specifically the Holocaust, became well-known. Darwinism had a profound negative influence in South Africa for over half a century. The fact is, a well-documented connection exists between Darwinism's child "'scientific racism,' and the entrenchment of white supremacy."[113] Darwinism produced a worldview that led to ascribing the traits and destiny of entire people groups based on the false claims of so-called "race science."[114]

In the early twentieth century, South Africa was no exception to this trend. The "science" of eugenics, conceived from Darwinism, became a convenient government tool in South Africa to pursue policies that were socially and politically useful to the White population. Government-supported educational and scientific bodies became the vehicles to provide the intellectual support for the racially discriminatory South African policies.

Thirty years after the birth of multiracial politics in South Africa, Darwinian influences still remain.[115] In 1994, the new South African government, to avoid being labeled "unscientific," embraced teaching evolution dogmatically in schools and universities. Like much of the rest of the Western world, the biblical creation belief is vehemently opposed and ridiculed in South Africa.[116] Despite the overwhelming evidence against evolution, it continues to be defended even by a few who claim to be Bible-believing Christians.[117]

112. Meredith, *Fortunes of Africa*, 481–87.

113. Dubow, *Science and Society*, 165.

114. Dubow, *Scientific Racism*, 98.

115. Gewald, *Herero Heroes*.

116. Dubow, *Scientific Racism*, 291.

117. Applegate and Stump, *How I Changed My Mind*.

So-called "Enlightenment" thinking led to the "emergence of natural history as a distinctive field of knowledge[, which] posed a formidable challenge to the traditional biblical account of common descent from Adam," and, quoting Professor Mosse, provided for "the rationalization of old prejudices."[118] In stark contrast, the biblical view is that God "made from one man every nation of mankind,"[119] and therefore, all men were, and are, equal before their Creator.

This science was not the result of experiment but from a desire to support secularism by promoting naturalism. To this end, science and the state were often mutually willing partners in developing governmental mandates. Furthermore, genocide has a long history and has involved scores of countries.[120] One thing all of these horrible events have in common is the rejection of the Genesis teaching that all humans are brothers and rejection of the teaching of Christ that all humans are our neighbors. And Christ commanded that we are to love our neighbor as ourselves. As Gilbert Keith Chesterton wrote almost a century ago, Darwinism was a "disputed system of thought which began with Evolution and has ended in Eugenics."[121] The most accurate summary of this chapter is as follows:

> We [the Europeans] have usurped their [the Africans'] lands, [and have] kidnapped, enslaved, and murdered them [the native Africans]. The greatest of their crimes is that they sometimes trespass into the lands of their forefathers, and the very greatest of their misfortunes is that they have ever become acquainted with Christians. Shame on such Christianity.[122]

118. Dubow, *Scientific Racism*, 25.

119. Acts 17:26, ESV.

120. Chalk and Jonassohn, *History and Sociology of Genocide*.

121. Chesterton, *Eugenics and Other Evils*, 77.

122. Brantlinger, *Dark Vanishings*, 74.

Other Books by Jerry Bergman

Teaching About Creation/Evolution Controversy
Bloomington, IN: Phi Delta Kappa Educational Foundation,
October 1979

"Peer Evaluation of University Faculty"
College Student Journal Monograph, 14(3), Part 2
Chula Vista, Fall 1980

Understanding Educational Measurement and Evaluation
Boston: Houghton Mifflin, 1981

The Criterion: Religious Discrimination in America
Richfield, MN: Onesimus, 1984
Worldcat lists 43 libraries with a copy.

*"Vestigial Organs" Are Fully Functional: A History and Evaluation
of the Vestigial Organ Origins Concept*
Terre Haute, IN: Creation Research Society, 1990

Ward's Science Lab Safety Manual
Rochester, NY: Ward's Natural Science, 2002

Persuaded by the Evidence
Edited with Doug Sharp
Green Forest, AR: Master, 2008

OTHER BOOKS BY JERRY BERGMAN

Slaughter of the Dissidents: The Shocking Truth About Killing the Careers of Darwin Doubters
Southworth, WA: Leafcutter, 2012

Hitler and the Nazi Darwinian Worldview: How the Nazi Eugenic Crusade for a Superior Race Caused the Greatest Holocaust in World History
Kitchener, Ont.: Joshua, 2012

Transformed by the Evidence
Edited with Doug Sharp
Southworth, WA: Leafcutter, 2014

The Darwin Effect: Its influence on Nazism, Eugenics, Racism, Communism, Capitalism, and Sexism
Green Forest, AR: Master, 2014

The Dark Side of Darwin
Green Forest, AR: New Leaf, 2015

C. S. Lewis: Anti-Darwinist: A Careful Examination of the Development of His Views on Darwinism
Eugene, OR: Wipf & Stock, 2016

Silencing the Darwin Skeptics
Southworth, WA: Leafcutter Press, 2016

How Darwinism Corrodes Morality: Darwinism, Immorality, Abortion, and the Sexual Revolution
Kitchener, Ont.: Joshua, 2017

Evolution's Blunders, Frauds, and Forgeries
Atlanta: CMI, 2017

Censoring the Darwin Skeptics: How Belief in Evolution is Enforced by Eliminating Dissidents
Southworth, WA: Leafcutter, 2018

Evolution is the Doorway to Atheism
Southworth, WA: Leafcutter, 2019

Science is the Doorway to Creation: Nobel Laureates and Other Eminent Scientists Who Reject Orthodox Darwinism
Southworth, WA: Leafcutter, 2019

God in President Eisenhower's Life, Military Career, and Presidency
Eugene, OR: Wipf & Stock, 2019

Darwinian Eugenics and the Holocaust: American Industrial Involvement
Peterborough, Ont.: Involgo, 2020

The Methodist Darwin Syndrome: Consequences of Adopting Darwinian Theology
Lansing, MI: Looking Glass River, 2021

Three Pillars of Evolution Demolished: Why Darwin Was Wrong
Bloomington, IN: WestBow, a division of Thomas Nelson and Zondervan, 2022

Debunking Human Evolution Taught in Our Public Schools: A Guidebook for Christian Students, Parents, and Pastors
with Dr. Daniel Bisbee
Folsom, CA: Genesis Apologetics, 2023

The Other Side of the Scopes Monkey Trial: At Its Heart the Trial Was About Racism
Eugene, OR: Wipf & Stock, 2023

OTHER BOOKS BY JERRY BERGMAN

Why Did God Create Viruses, Bacteria, and Other Pathogens
Bloomington, IN: WestBow, a division of Thomas Nelson and
Zondervan, 2023

C. S. Lewis' War Against Scientism and Naturalism
Jordan Station, Ont.: Cantaro, 2023

*Evolution's Dangerous Ideas: Eugenics, Lobotomies, Using X-Rays
to Speed Up Evolution, and Other Dangerous Ideas Inspired by
Darwinism*
Jordan Station, Ont.: Cantaro, 2024

Tackling Tough Issues
Grand Rapids: Red Cedar, 2024

*Useless Organs: The Rise and Fall of the Once Major Argument for
Evolution*
Revised edition, Creation Summit, 2025

The "Poor Design" Argument Against Intelligent Design Falsified
Revised edition, Creation Summit, 2025

Fossil Forensics: Separating Fact from Fantasy in Paleontology
Revised edition, Creation Summit, 2025

About the Author

Professor Bergman taught at the college level for over forty-five years. He served on both the undergraduate and graduate faculty at Bowling Green State University, the University of Toledo, and the Medical College of Ohio. His nine earned degrees include a doctorate from Wayne State University in Detroit, Michigan, a master's of science in biomedical science, a master's in occupational health, and a master's of public health from the Medical College of Ohio. After completing his medical education, he was hired full-time doing cancer research in the Department of Experimental Pathology at the Medical College of Ohio.

The 1,026 college credit hours he has earned is the equivalent to almost twenty master's degrees. An award-winning author, Dr. Bergman has over fourteen hundred publications in both scholarly and popular science journals. His work has been translated into thirteen languages, including French, German, Italian, Spanish, Danish, Arabic, Russian, Polish, Turkish, and Swedish. His books, and books that include chapters he authored, are in over fifteen hundred college libraries in twenty-eight countries. So far, over eighty thousand copies of the fifty-one books and monographs that he has authored or coauthored are in print.

His writings include a fastback on the creation-evolution controversy published by the honor society in education, Phi Delta Kappa. He also published a college textbook on evaluation with Houghton Mifflin and has contributed chapters to numerous others. His books include *Fossil Forensics: Separating Fact from*

Fantasy in Paleontology and *Darwinism's Blunders, Frauds and Forgeries*, all available from Amazon.com and other bookstores.

Dr. Bergman has presented over one hundred scientific papers at professional meetings. His research has made the front page in newspapers throughout the country five times and was featured by Paul Harvey several times on national radio. He was a featured speaker on over one thousand college campuses and churches in North America, Africa, Asia, and Europe and is also a frequent guest on various radio and television programs. During his teaching career, Professor Bergman was awarded outstanding teacher twice.

Bibliography

Alozie, Bright. "Space and Colonial Alterity: Interrogating British Residential Segregation in Nigeria, 1899–1919." *Ufahamu: A Journal of African Studies* 41.2 (2020) 5. https://doi.org/10.5070/F7412046832.

Ambler, Marc. "Herero Genocide." *Creation* 27.3 (2005) 52–55.

Anderson, Austin. "The Dark Side of Darwinism." *Philosophy for the Many* (blog), Nov. 16, 2016. https://sites.williams.edu/engl-209-fall16/uncategorized /the-dark-side-of-darwinism/.

Andersson, N. "Tuberculosis and Social Stratification in South Africa." *International Journal of Health Services* 20.1 (1990) 141–65. https:// pubmed.ncbi.nlm.nih.gov/2307553/.

André, Charles. "Phrenology and the Rwandan Genocide." *Arquivos de Neuro-Psiquiatria* 76.4 (April 2018) 277–82. https://www.researchgate.net/ publication/324972132_Phrenology_and_the_Rwandan_Genocide/ figures?lo=1.

Anele, Uzonna. "These African Countries Are Still Awaiting Restitution of the French Army's Crimes and Return of Wealth Looted from Their Lands." Talk Africana, Dec. 16, 2020. https://talkafricana.com/these-african-countries-are-still-awaiting-restitution-of-the-french-armys-crimes-and-return-of-wealth-looted-from-their-lands/.

Anstey, Roger. *King Leopold's Legacy: The Congo Under Belgian Rule 1908–1960.* Oxford: Oxford University Press, 1966.

Applegate, Kathryn, and J. B. Stump. *How I Changed My Mind About Evolution: Evangelicals Reflect on Faith and Science.* Downers Grove, IL: IVP Academic, 2016.

Arnold, Guy. *Africa: A Modern History.* London: Atlantic, 2005.

Arnold, Michael. *Imperial Atrocities: Skeletons in Colonial Closets.* Houston: Strategic, 2022.

Ascherson, Neal. *The King Incorporated: Leopold the Second and the Congo.* London: Granta, 2001.

Associated Press. "Belgium's Colonial-Era King Leopold Faces Reckoning as Anti-racism Protests Grow." *Los Angeles Times*, June 11, 2020. https://

www.latimes.com/world-nation/story/2020-06-11/belgian-king-leopold-faces-reckoning-anti-racism-protests.

Bainton, Roland. *Christian Attitudes Toward War and Peace.* Nashville: Abingdon, 1960.

Banks, Nick. "Mixed-Race Children and Families." In *Meeting the Needs of Ethnic Minority Children: Including Refugee, Black, and Mixed Parentage Children,* 2nd ed., edited by Kedar Nath Dwivedi, 219–32. London: Jessica Kingsley, 2002.

Barker, Martin. *The New Racism: Conservatives and the Ideology of the Tribe.* Carlton, MN: N. P. Junction, 1981.

Barta, Tony. "Mr. Darwin's Shooters: On Natural Selection and the Naturalizing of Genocide." *Patterns of Prejudice* 39.2 (2005) 116–37. https://doi.org/10.1080/00313220500106170.

Bartrop, Paul R. *Encountering Genocide: Personal Accounts from Victims, Perpetrators, and Witnesses.* Santa Barbara, CA: ABC-CLIO, 2014.

Beinart, William, and Saul Dubow. *The Scientific Imagination in South Africa: 1700 to the Present.* Cambridge: Cambridge University Press, 2021.

Belgium ministère des affaires africaines. *Rapport sur de l'administration belge du Ruanda-Urundi, 1925.* Brussels: Ministère, 1925.

Bell, Frank W. "The African Society." *South Africa Magazine,* Jan. 23, 1909.

Birt, Whitaker R. *The Congo: From Leopold to Lumumba.* Stanford: Stanford University Press, 2017.

Bishop, George. "The Religious Worldview and American Beliefs About Human Origins." *Public Perspective* 9.4 (1998) 39–44.

Blanchard, Pascal, et al., eds. *Human Zoos: Science and Spectacle in the Age of Colonial Empires.* Liverpool: Liverpool University Press, 2008.

Blumenbach, Johann. *On the Natural Variety of Mankind.* New York: Bergman, 1969.

Borstelmann, Thomas. *Apartheid's Reluctant Uncle: The United States and Southern Africa in the Early Cold War.* New York: Oxford University Press, 1993.

Brantlinger, Patrick. *Dark Vanishings: Discourse on the Extinction of Primitive Races, 1800–1930.* Ithaca, NY: Cornell University Press, 2015.

Brenan, Megan. "Majority Still Credits God for Humankind, but Not Creationism." Gallup, July 22, 2024. https://news.gallup.com/poll/647594/majority-credits-god-humankind-not-creationism.aspx.

Brigham, Albert Perry, and Charles T. McFarlane. *Essentials of Geography: First Book.* New York: American, 1916.

Burrell, Kevin. "Slavery, the Hebrew Bible and the Development of Racial Theories in the Nineteenth Century." *Religions* 12.9 (2021) 742. https://doi.org/10.3390/rel12090742.

Campbell, John, and Matthew T. Page. *Nigeria: What Everyone Needs to Know.* New York: Oxford University Press, 2018.

Carroll, Al. *Survivors: Family Histories of Surviving, War, Capitalism, and Genocide.* Morrisville, NC: Lulu, 2016.

Cell, John. *The Highest Stage of White Supremacy*. New York: Cambridge University Press, 1982.

Chalk, Frank, and Kurt Jonassohn. *The History and Sociology of Genocide*. New Haven, CT: Yale University Press, 1990.

Chesterton, G. K. *Eugenics and Other Evils*. London: Cassel, 1922.

Chorover, Stephan L. *Genesis to Genocide: The Meaning of Human Nature*. Cambridge, MA: MIT Press, 1979.

Claeys, Gregory, ed. *The Cambridge Companion to Nineteenth-Century Thought*. Cambridge: Cambridge University Press, 2019.

Cohen, William B. *The French Encounter with Africans: White Response to Blacks, 1530–1880*. Bloomington, IN: Indiana University Press, 1980.

Cronjé, Geoffrey. *'n Tuiste vir die Nageslag* [A home for our descendants]. Pretoria: University of South Africa, 1945.

Darwin, Charles. *Charles Darwin: His Life Told in an Autobiographical Chapter*. New York: D. Appleton, 1893.

———. *The Descent of Man, and Selection in Relation to Sex*. London: John Murray, 1871.

———. *The Descent of Man, and Selection in Relation to Sex*. 2nd ed. London: John Murray, 1874.

———. *Journal of Researches*. 2nd ed. London: John Murray, 1845.

———. *On the Origin of Species by Means of Natural Selection, or the Preservation of Favoured Races in the Struggle for Life*. London: John Murray, 1859.

Darwin Correspondence Project. "From William Henry Harvey 24 August 1860." https://www.darwinproject.ac.uk/letter?docId=letters/DCP-LETT-2898.xml.

———. "From William Preyer 27 April 1871." https://www.darwinproject. ac.uk/letter/?docId=letters/DCP-LETT-7721.xml.

Decker, Corrie, and Elisabeth McMahon. *The Idea of Development in Africa: A History*. New York: Cambridge University Press, 2021.

Dennis, Rutledge M. "Social Darwinism, Scientific Racism, and the Metaphysics of Race." *The Journal of Negro Education* 64.3 (1995) 243–52.

Desmond, Adrian, and James Moore. *Darwin's Sacred Cause*. London: Penguin, 2009.

Dickins, Peter. "The 'BLACK' Concentration Camps of the Boer War." The Observation Post: South African Military History, Sept. 3, 2017. https:// samilhistory.com/2017/09/03/to-fully-reconcile-the-boer-war-is-to-fully-understand-the-black-concentration-camps/.

Dubow, Saul, ed. *Science and Society in Southern Africa (Studies in Imperialism)*. New York: Manchester University Press, 2000.

———. *Scientific Racism in Modern South Africa*. Cambridge: Cambridge University Press, 1995.

Duerden, J. E. "Genetics and Eugenics in South African Heredity and Environment." *South African Journal of Science* 22.11 (1925) 59–72. https://hdl.handle.net/10520/AJA00382353_8556.

Dworkin, Ira. *Congo Love Song: African American Culture and the Crisis of the Colonial State.* Chapel Hill, NC: University of North Carolina Press, 2017.

Egan, John. "Hitler and the Social Construction of Reality." *6 Million and Counting.* http://www.6millionandcounting.com/files/Reality.html.

Elkins, Caroline. *Imperial Reckoning: The Untold Story of Britain's Gulag in Kenya.* New York: Henry Holt, 2005.

———. *Legacy of Violence. A History of the British Empire.* New York: Vintage, 2023.

Encyclopaedia Britannica. "Herero Genocide." Chicago: Encyclopedia Britannica, 1957.

Encyclopaedia Britannica Online. "Arthur de Gobineau." Oct. 9, 2025. https://www.britannica.com/biography/Arthur-de-Gobineau.

Falola, Toyin, and Matthew M. Heaton. *A History of Nigeria.* New York: Cambridge University Press, 2008.

Fredrickson, George M. *The Black Image in the White Mind: The Debate on Afro-American Character and Destiny, 1817–1914.* Hanover, NH: Wesleyan University Press, 1971.

Gallois, William. *A History of Violence in the Early Algerian Colony.* London: Palgrave Macmillan, 2013.

Gewald, Jan-Bart. *Herero Heroes: A Socio-Political History of the Herero of Namibia 1890–1923.* Oxford: James Currey, 1999.

Gilbert, F., et al. "Ethnic Intermarriage and Its Consequences for Cystic Fibrosis Carrier Screening." *American Journal of Preventative Medicine* 11.4 (1995) 251–55. https://pubmed.ncbi.nlm.nih.gov/7495602/.

Glick, Thomas F., ed. *The Comparative Reception of Darwinism.* Austin: University of Texas Press, 1963.

Goddard, Henry H. *The Kallikak Family. A Study in the Heredity of Feeble-Mindedness.* New York, NY: Macmillan, 1912.

Goineau, Arthur de. *Essay on the Inequality of the Human Races, 1853–1855.* London: William Heineman, 1915.

Goldman, Charles Sydney, ed. *The Empire and the Century: A Series of Essays on Imperial Problems and Possibilities.* London: John Murray, 1905.

Graeber, David, and David Wengrow. *The Dawn of Everything: A New History of Humanity.* New York: Farrar, Straus, and Giroux, 2021.

Grad, Charles. *L'Alsace: Le pays et ses habitants.* Strasbourg, FR: Contades, 1889.

Hamel, Chouki El. *Black Morocco: A History of Slavery, Race, and Islam.* New York: Cambridge University Press, 2013.

Harari, Yuval Noah. *Sapiens: A Brief History of Humankind.* New York: HarperCollins, 2015.

Hasian, Marouf, Jr. "The 'Hysterical' Emily Hobhouse and Boer War Concentration Camp Controversy." *Western Journal of Communication* 67.2 (2003) 138–63. https://doi.org/10.1080/10570310309374764.

Hawkins, B. Waterhouse. *Comparative Anatomy Applied to the Purpose of the Artist.* London: Windsor & Newton, 1883.

Hays, Benjamin K. "Natural Selection and the Race Problem." *Charlotte Medical Journal* (May 1905) 1–21.

Hinman, Russell. *Eclectic Physical Geography*. New York: American, 1888.

Hinton, Alexander Laban. *Why Did They Kill? Cambodia in the Shadow of Genocide*. Berkeley: University of California Press, 2003.

Hochschild, Adam. *King Leopold's Ghost*. New York: Mariner, 1999.

Howard, R. T. "Revolt in Madagascar." History Today, Mar. 29, 2017. https://www.historytoday.com/history-matters/revolt-madagascar.

Janse, A. J. "White and Black in South Africa." *Transvaal Educational News* 25 (1928) 9.

JBHE Foundation. "Blacks Less Likely to Accept Charles Darwin's Dethronement of Mankind." *The Journal of Blacks in Higher Education* 21 (1998) 39–40. https://doi.org/10.2307/2998974.

Jean, Moise. "The Rwandan Genocide: The True Motivations for Mass Killings." Scribd. https://www.scribd.com/document/35166915/The-Rwandan-Genocide-True-Motivations-for-Mass-Killings-By-Moise-Jean.

Johnson, S. D. "Darwin's Legacy in South African Evolutionary Biology." *South African Journal of Science* 105.11–12 (2009) 403–9. https://scielo.org.za/scielo.php?script=sci_arttext&pid=S0038-23532009000600009.

Johnson, Todd M., and Peter F. Crossing. "Religions by Continent." *Journal of Religion and Demography* 9.1–2 (2022) 91–110. doi:10.1163/2589742x-bja10013.

Jones, Adam. *Genocide: A Comprehensive Introduction*. New York: Routledge, 2006.

Joy, Jessica. "Western Influence, Latent Racism, and Their Impact on Access to Health Care in Madagascar." Independent Study Project (ISP) Collection 1099 (2011). https://digitalcollections.sit.edu/isp_collection/1099.

Keith, Arthur. *Evolution and Ethics*. New York: G.P. Putnams's Sons, 1947.

Kellogg, Vernon. *Headquarter Nights: A Record of Conversations and Experiences at the Headquarters of the German Army in France and Belgium*. Boston: Atlantic Monthly, 1917.

Kendi, Ibram X. *Stamped from the Beginning: The Definitive History of Racist Ideas in America*. New York: Bold Type, 2016.

Keynes, R. D., ed. *Charles Darwin's Beagle Diary*. Cambridge: Cambridge University Press, 1988.

Kiernan, Ben. *Blood and Soil: A World History of Genocide and Extermination from Sparta to Darfur*. New Haven, CT: Yale University Press, 2007.

Kolapo, Femi J. *Christian Missionary Engagement in Central Nigeria, 1857–1891*. London: Palgrave Macmillan, 2019.

Koorts, Lindie. *DF Malan and the Rise of Afrikaner Nationalism*. Cape Town: Tafelberg, 2014.

Langbehn, Volker, and Mohammad Salama, eds. *German Colonialism: Race, the Holocaust, and Postwar Germany*. New York: Columbia University Press, 2011.

Latson, Jennifer. "The Biracial Advantage." *Psychology Today*, May 7, 2019. https://www.psychologytoday.com/us/articles/201905/the-biracial-advantage.

Lerner, Richard. *Final Solutions: Biology, Prejudice, and Genocide*. University Park, PA: Pennsylvania State University Press, 1992.

Lindqvist, Sven. *Exterminate All the Brutes: One Man's Odyssey into the Heart of Darkness and the Origins of European Genocide*. Translated by Joan Tate. New York: New Press, 1996.

Liston, Zachary. "Basis of Social Darwinism and the Herero Genocide." Science, Technology, and Society, Oct. 25, 2020. https://web.colby.edu/st112a-fall20/2020/10/25/basis-of-social-darwinism-and-the-herero-genocide/.

Little, Anthony C., et al. "Facial Attractiveness: Evolutionary-Based Research." *Philosophical Transactions of the Royal Society* 366.1571 (2011) 1638–59. https://doi.org/10.1098/rstb.2010.0404.

Lugard, Frederick. *The Dual Mandate on the British Tropical Africa*. Edinburgh: William Blackwood and Sons, 1922.

Luthuli, Albert. *Let My People Go*. New York: McGraw Hill, 2006.

Maitland, Alexander. *Speke: And the Discovery of the Source of the Nile*. Limited ed. London: Faber & Faber, 2010.

Mamdani, Mahmood. *When Victims Become Killers: Colonialism, Nativism, and the Genocide*. Princeton, NJ: Princeton University Press, 2001.

Manzo, Kathryn A. *Creating Boundaries: The Politics of Race and Nation*. Boulder, CO: Lynne Rienner, 1996.

Maran, Rita. *Torture: The Role of Ideology in the French-Algerian War*. New York: Praeger, 1989.

Marney, Carlyle. *Structures of Prejudice*. New York: Abingdon, 1961.

Mathews, Basil. *The Book of Missionary Heroes*. N.p.: CreateSpace, 2015.

Marx, Anthony W. *Making Race and Nation: A Comparison of the United States, South Africa, and Brazil*. New York: Cambridge University Press, 1998.

McDougall, James. *A History of Algeria*. Cambridge: Cambridge University Press, 2017.

McGregor, Danae. "German and American Eugenics in the Pre-World War I Era." *Answers Research Journal* 6 (2013) 71–77.

Melvern, Linda. *A People Betrayed: The Role of the West in Rwanda's Genocide*. New York: Zed, 2000.

Mentan, Tatah. *Recurrent Genocidal Nightmares: The Hidden Side of Euro-African Encounters, 1450–1950*. Bemenda, CM: Langaa, 2019.

Meredith, Martin. *The Fortunes of Africa: A 5000-Year History of Wealth, Greed, and Endeavor*. New York: Public Affairs, 2014.

Millar, Henry. "Racism in Rwanda." Centre for Ethnicity and Racism Studies (CERS) Working Paper, University of Leeds, 2014. https://cers.leeds.ac.uk/wp-content/uploads/sites/97/2015/01/Racism-in-Rwanda.pdf.

Morel, E. D. *King Leopold's Rule in Africa*. New York: Praeger, 1971.

Moses, A. Dirk, ed. *Empire, Colony, Genocide: Conquest, Occupation, and Subaltern Resistance in World History*. New York: Berghahn, 2010.

Moses, A. Dirk, and Dan Stone, eds. *Colonialism and Genocide*. New York: Routledge, 2007.

Muhammad, Maryam Salihu, et al. "A Review of Residential Segregation and Its Consequences in Nigeria." *Mediterranean Journal of Social Sciences* 6.2 (March 2015) 376–84.

Nasrallah, Farid. "Documented Examples of French Crimes in Algeria in the 19th century." *Social Sciences and Humans Review* 17.2 (2024) 71–89.

Ndahiro, Kennedy. "Dehumanization: How Tutsis Were Reduced to Cockroaches, Snakes to Be Killed." *New Times*, Mar. 13, 2014. https://www.newtimes.co.rw/section/read/73836.

Neba-Fuh, Emmanuel. *Triumph of Racism: The History of White Supremacy in Africa and How Shithole Entered the US Presidential Lexicon*. Kansas City, MO: Miraclaire, 2021.

Nzongola-Ntalaja, Georges. *The Congo from Leopold to Kabila: A People's History*. London: Zed, 2013.

Oluniyi, Olufemi. "The Cruel Legacy of Social Darwinism in Nigeria." *Science & Culture Today*, Feb. 21, 2023. https://scienceandculture.com/2023/02/the-cruel-legacy-of-social-darwinism-in-nigeria/.

———. *Darwin Comes to Africa: Social Darwinism and British Imperialism in Northern Nigeria*. Seattle: Discovery Institute, 2023.

Olusoga, David, and Casper W. Erichsen. *The Kaiser's Holocaust: Germany's Forgotten Genocide and the Colonial Roots of Nazism*. London: Faber & Faber, 2011.

Panné, Jean-Louis, et al. *The Black Book of Communism: Crimes, Terror, Repression*. Cambridge: Harvard University Press, 1999.

Pretorius, Fransjohan. "The Boer Wars." BBC, Mar. 29, 2011. https://www.bbc.co.uk/history/british/victorians/boer_wars_01.shtml.

Prunier, Gérard. *The Rwanda Crisis: History of a Genocide*. New York: Columbia University Press, 1995.

Reade, W. Winwood. *The Martyrdom of Man*. London: Trübner, 1872.

———. *Savage Africa: Being the Narrative of a Tour in Equatorial, Southwestern, and Northwestern Africa*. New York: Harper & Brothers, 1864.

Rich, Paul. "Race, Science, and the Legitimization of White Supremacy in South Africa, 1902–1940." *International Journal of African Historical Studies* 23.4 (1990) 665–86.

Rotberg, Robert I. *The Founder: Cecil Rhodes and the Pursuit of Power*. New York: Oxford University Press, 1988.

Saada, Emmanuelle. *Empire's Children: Race, Filiation, and Citizenship in the French Colonies*. Translated by Arthur Goldhammer. Chicago: University of Chicago Press, 2012.

Sarkin, Jeremy. *Colonial Genocide and Reparations Claims in the 21st Century: The Socio-Legal Context of Claims Under International Law by the Hero Against Germany for Genocide in Namibia, 1904–1908*. Westport, CT: Praeger Security International, 2009.

Savage, Susannah. "From Slavery to Indenture: Race and Culture Amongst Indians in French Colonial Plantation Societies, 1750–1888." PhD diss., University of London, 2025. https://doi.org/10.25501/SOAS.00043729.

Scholtz, Leopold. *Why the Boers Lost the War*. London: Palgrave-Macmillan, 2005.

Scholz, William, ed. *The Phenomenon of Torture: Readings and Commentary*. Philadelphia: University of Pennsylvania Press, 2007.

Shufeldt, Robert W. *America's Greatest Problem: The Negro*. Philadelphia: F. A. Davis, 1915.

Sindani, Jeanne-Marie. *Gestrandet im "Paradies."* Friedberg im Breisgau, DE: Lambertus-Verlag, 2018.

Sinema, Kyrsten. *Who Must Die in Rwanda's Genocide? The State of Exception Realized*. Lanham, MD: Lexington, 2015.

Smith, J. David. *Minds Made Feeble: The Myth and Legacy of the Kallikaks*. Rockville, MD: Aspen, 1985.

Smith, William Benjamin. *The Color Line: A Brief in Behalf of the Unborn*. New York: McClure, Phillips, 1905.

Steinwehr, Adolph von, and Daniel Brinton. *Primary Geography, Eclectic Series, Number One*. Cincinnati: Van Antwerp, Bragg, 1870.

Stocking, George W., Jr. *Race, Culture, and Evolution: Essays in the History of Anthropology*. Chicago: University of Chicago Press, 1982.

Straus, Scott. *The Order of Genocide: Race, Power, and War in Rwanda*. Ithaca, NY: Cornell University Press, 2006.

Sultanov, Kerim. "Nuclear Nightmares and Colonial Crimes: France's Unforgiven Historical Sins." News.AZ, July 10, 2024. https://news.az/news/nuclear-nightmares-and-colonial-crimes-frances-unforgiven-historical-sins-analysis.

Thompson, Ian. "The Kaiser's Holocaust by David Olusoga and Casper W Erichsen: Review." *The Telegraph*, Aug. 16, 2010. https://www.telegraph.co.uk/culture/books/bookreviews/7940763/The-Kaisers-Holocaust-by-David-Olusoga-and-Casper-W-Erichsen-review.html.

Tobach, Ethel, et al. *The Four Horsemen: Racism, Sexism, Militarism and Social Darwinism*. New York: Behavioral, 1974.

Totten, Samuel, and Robert K. Hitchcock, eds. *Genocide of Indigenous Peoples: A Critical Bibliographic Review*. New York: Routledge, 2017.

Turner, Carla. "The Eugenic Underpinnings of Apartheid South Africa, and Its Influence on the South African School System." *Theoria: A Journal of Social and Political Theory* 71.178 (2024) 75–95. https://doi.org/10.3167/th.2024.7117804.

Twagilimana, Amiable. *The Debris of Ham: Ethnicity, Regionalism, and the 1994 Rwandan Genocide*. Lanham, MD: University Press of Maryland, 2003.

Twain, Mark. *King Leopold's Soliloquy*. Boston: R. Warren, 1905.

Wamwere, Koigi Wa. *Negative Ethnicity: From Bias to Genocide*. New York: Seven Stories, 2023.

Wikipedia. "List of Wars by Death Toll." May 27, 2025. https://en.wikipedia.org/wiki/List_of_wars_by_death_toll.

Wonkam, Ambroise. "Perspectives in Genomics and Sickle Cell Disease Therapeutics." In *Molecular Hematology*, 5th ed., edited by Drew Provan and Hillard M. Lazarus, 187–200. New York: Wiley, 2024. https://doi.org/10.1002/9781394180486.ch14.

Wood, Bernard Anthony. "Paleo-Anthropology's Superstar." *American Scientist* 112.6 (2024) 326–27.

Yudell, Michael. *Race Unmasked: Biology and Race in the Twentieth Century.* New York: Columbia University Press, 2014.

Zubrin, Robert. *Merchants of Despair: Radical Environmentalists, Criminal Pseudo-Scientists, and the Fatal Cult of Antihumanism.* New York: Encounter, 2012.

www.ingramcontent.com/pod-product-compliance
Lightning Source LLC
Chambersburg PA
CBHW061047250726

48653CB00001B/296